EXOTIC ART

Exotic

SPRING BOOKS
LONDON

Art——

W. & B. Forman

EDITED BY LUBOR HÁJEK
INTRODUCED BY V. V. ŠTECH
WITH ARTICLES BY
B. FORMAN · L. HÁJEK · Z. ŽÁBA
J. HLOUCHA · V. ŠOLC · N. FRÝD
A. HOFFMEISTER · M. OPLT

Designed and produced by Artia for
SPRING BOOKS
Spring House · Spring Place · London NW 5
Printed in Czechoslovakia

CONTENTS

FOREWORD

The main function of an artistic work, even one not directly created for us but for people of other ages and climes, is to give pleasure. Thus it does not merely exist for purposes of study, classification, cataloguing or to teach us something. This obvious fact is unfortunately too often forgotten. Even private collectors have reached the point where they classify their collections more than love them, gradually losing their right to the name of "amateur" or at least disowning the meaning of this word.

Our introductory assertion that an artistic work has the main function of pleasing is given as a statement of programme. It formed the initial impulse and guide to all working on this book who had made up their minds to share with the broad reading public the joy and healthy pleasure obtainable from the artistic works of various nations and ages. No narrower framework was set. We concentrated generally on works originating outside Europe, the works of individual and closed groups, creative works both old and new, canonical and popular, historically important and unimportant—in other words, just as we came across them in the public and private collections of this country.

The result of our work has thus slightly the form of a symposium, a classic banquet to which the collectors brought their symbolæ, contributions chosen according to what each had at home, what each liked and what each wished to share with the others.

Naturally such a banquet must be forgiven for not being unified and systematic. It cannot be a work constructed and produced with discrimination, an exhaustive encyclopædic tome. The gifts brought with love to the common table are not always representative examples of a certain artistic sphere just as the individual spheres are not proportionally represented and many chapters could not be included at all (e.g. monumental sculpture, glass from Asia Minor, the painting of China, Japan and India, the ceramics of the Far East, etc.). But one certainly feels pleasure in the beauty, the infinite and diverse creative powers of humanity, and in the freedom and discipline which go into a great work of art. Some information is given on the artistic forms of the accepted great works of art and on the beauty of the less pretentious and less obvious, and here and there are contributions for the expert and the possibility of studying objects not yet made public.

As for the texts—these were also brought in the form of a symposium. They could not be, nor did they aim at being exhaustive and uniform. In an attempt to introduce at least the flicker of an explanation into the sections entrusted to them the various authors chose their own methods according to the dictates of their consciences. One concentrated on factual information, another chose the form of essay, a third discussed a point on the margin of the subject, yet another limited himself to one or two examples of reproductions. One brought something to satisfy the average reader, another hurried in with information interesting to the expert.

The principle that an artistic work is there to give us pleasure was also the guiding rule in the question of photographic work. It cannot be denied that reproductions (particularly of sculptural works) do not present to us the object itself but only one aspect of it, conditioned by a certain lighting. Reproductions cannot be

IX

made without lighting. One cannot take refuge in so-called neutral lighting as some like to do, for this too is one type of lighting. We thus decided to follow the principle of optimum lighting which brings out the best artistic qualities including the surface quality of the material, to choose a lighting which shows the typical characteristics of the work being reproduced. We decided to avoid the temptation of reproducing effective but unrealistic lighting which does not bring out the thing itself—and likewise to avoid unrealistic neutral lighting. It would be hard to find a work (particularly in the art of Africa, India, etc.) intended by the artist for this neutral lighting of a room in November. He certainly more often counted on illumination expressed more clearly, dramatically or even with a certain atmosphere which unfortunately we can only gropingly produce if we wish to satisfy the requirements of realism.

The ambition of the authors of this book, however, was not only to impart to the readers the principal and characteristic properties of the objects chosen, to show them the object itself, but to show them the reason why they may derive pleasure from the object, why they may like it. There is no doubt that this is no easy task since in their origin, content and form, these works of art are foreign to our deep-rooted and accustomed conceptions and criteria. Difference in conceptions and criteria is sometimes an equal impediment to mutual understanding, respect and friendly relations among the nations of the world. This can be removed by understanding and learning, and above all by love. One cannot be indifferent to a nation the art of which one likes and one cannot but desire friendship among all countries if one likes the art of all countries. If this book is able to contribute its mite in this aspect, then we can proudly say that it has fulfilled its task.

L. H.

INTRODUCTION

The world of remote forms—could be the sub-title of this book. Or better still, *worlds*, for from the conglomeration of ethnographic documents brought back by Czech travellers, from the tools, decorations, objects, curiosities and art works amassed by collectors, there emerges to the unethnographic glance a conception of several different economic, philosophical and political systems. Things complex as well as simple tell us of nations with a long history, of nations whose past cannot be clearly discerned, of geographical and ethnical continuity. They record the first struggle for life and the complicated civilisations and cultures down through the ages. With their curious magic they allure our fantasy to wander through the world and ages wherein we meet with man and humanity in numerous forms and at different stages of development.

Is it mere exoticism? It is indeed something more serious and powerful than mere fascination. In dealing with the forms of these objects which come from distant countries and peoples of various races and faiths, it opens up a perspective to the very beginning of time. In these forms are crystallized and preserved for us the by-gone conditions and driving force of life. In them man has endured and continues to speak in his inchoate consciousness of the external world, forever raising questions that defy a definitive answer, forever contemplating and interpreting life with a new revelation of order and form. We are accustomed to observe the art of foreign countries from a purely æsthetic point of view and to be moved by its strangeness or uniqueness. However, we need but delve into it a bit deeper to find beneath the surface a logic of its own, the reflection of a certain society with its material conditions and social structure, nature as seen by the creator of the object, and his personal and social feelings. They are intangible relations which cannot be rendered into exact scientific formulations. It is the subtle world of fancy continually in the process of creation from work, beliefs, desires, dreams and fears. It is a world based on experience and concrete reality yet transcending into a barely tangible and controllable sphere.

We sense and in fact do find behind the apparently curious and senseless things their reason, origin and sense. Beneath the outward appearance we can, with an effort, discern the idea-content which was once completely obvious to the society for which the object was created. There is no doubt that this material of the museums and collections once acted on collective feeling, forming the sub-conscious and expressing outlook on life. Today it is a proof of the human reactions to nature and life, a rare witness to the never-ending search for truth, to the never-ending process of vivification by which man from time immemorial transforms the vagueness of nature into forms expressive and definitive.

In the collection presented in this book we find various degrees of perfection and quality corresponding to the state of civilization of the ethnic unit concerned. There are evidences of the stages when it is still impossible to distinguish the concepts *to work* and *to create* so that it is with difficulty we distinguish between objects required and created by the needs of mere existence and works having no practical purpose but created as into a vacuum unconsciously under the impulse of an instinctive desire for expression. Things serving mere necessity become dead as soon as man discards them. Man uses them, strengthens himself with them, extends his domain and arms himself with them in the struggle with nature. In contrast, there are works which can be said to have a life of their own. The material used was in this case more or less transformed and took on a new meaning, becoming an enlivened body. Although an axe may seem to have been a form more living than a block of wood in primitive sculpture, it nevertheless acts in another sphere. It is an object for use and service, whereas a statue carries an inherent will to become animated and to give voice to the soul—by suggestion at least.

In the ethnographic collections some exhibits are complicated and full of fantasy while others are miserable, colourless and unattractive, the latter being for the most part documents of the beginnings of man's independence. They bear witness to the prehistoric society or the struggle of man with a stinting nature. It was a precarious and niggardly life, dependent on chance and the whims of the weather, that the natives of Baffin or other territories of the Arctic led. A mere piece of laboriously hewn stone, a carved bone pierced with a hole or ground to a point, already meant a kind of certainty for man. It was necessary to hunt for a suitable piece of stone, bone or wood, for these first tools and weapons, to chip the stone and fix the discovered gift of nature with a notch. Thus a harpoon was made from the bone, some kind of dress from the skin and the formless matter had changed into a thing belonging to man. By hollowing out a piece of wood a bowl was formed; a reindeer horn fastened to a branch or a stone attached to a stick produced a spear, hammer or fishing hook, needles and knives were obtained from parts of captured animals. In such a slow and laborious manner the man of prehistoric times or of not long ago freed himself from nature's hold. Man worked up a formless piece of raw material into tools, giving them his own scale; he mastered and limited material with regular outlines, thus distinguishing it from the rest of nature. He marked it with axes and edges, directions effected by the strength of his hand. He thus increased the possibilities of the object produced by purposive differentiation for piercing, cutting, scraping and other acts arising with the progress of technique.

Even in these simplest objects we observe an effort to bend nature to man's will by a symmetrical formal design, accent of shape or rhythmical division where the fundamental faculties of man—symmetry, proportion and rhythm—find expression. These are the organic results of the orderly movement of man's body which has two legs and arms, identical eyes and ears related to the central axis of the nose. His limbs are mutually proportional and from their composition arises an instinctive sense for proportionality. The life of the body is expressed by breath, pulse, voice and step in regularly repeated rhythmic order. These inborn properties of the organism, projected into the object created, appear as *decorativeness* which is fundamentally nothing more than the striving for complete mastery of the material, for such a finishing of the objects that they can be adapted for use. This decorativeness is thus at the very basis of work and not a thing apart. There are rhythmic elements in the mere expression of functional shapes; decorative value is simply the end product of an accomplished work whereby primitive man took possession of his environment.

In addition to such documents of primitive man's first struggle with nature there have been preserved in some primitive creations materialized impulses and direct reactions to the world which cannot be included in the sphere of utilitarian and regular human labour. These were stimulated by an instinct for expression. While the repetitive, constant labour originating in his physical constitution establishes the physical existence of man, the senses then arouse man's need to recognize the phenomenal world and to assert himself by means of song, dance and free creation. The documents of diluvial art give us an insight into the beginnings of this impulsive self-assertion. Such documents are those found in Věstonice and Předmostí or in the artifacts of some nations living until quite recently in conditions analogous to those which formed the oldest human society. There are for example the drawings and paintings of the South-African bushmen which were brought to Europe by the Czech explorer Dr. Emil Holub, and the sculptures and drawings of some Eskimo tribes. These drawings depict animals and people in such life-like movements and so accurately observed that they bear witness to unique pictorial memory. Shadow-like drawings done on rocks by irregular blows with a sharp piece of slate rendered remarkably concrete pictures. Visual perceptions were transformed into compact images without contours, intuitively and spatially rendering the momentary excitement. The realism of these perceptions can on'y be explained by the complete identification of the subject with the object – the animal depicted and the man who knew the animals intimately because his existence was based on this knowledge, on the sharpness of his senses and the ability for immediate orientation. The artist-hunter had to approach the hunted animal to such an extent that he projected himself into its life, identifying himself with it, and then registering it on the vibrating surface of the stone as the permanent record of experienced reality. In the bushmen's paintings the bodies of animals, originally extended out in space, were transposed into light relationships; whole complicated scenes were conceived as rapid sketches without points of accent. This was because they were the fruit of a constant, direct relationship to reality, to reality which was observed by the artist but remained inexplicable to him. It is pure *realism* rendered in memorized narration without a model. The art of the Chukchi Eskimos and other paleoarctic tribes has the same features. These inhabitants of the inhospitable north also comprehend animals and people in all their complexity: a walking man, a walrus, reindeer, bear or duck are done in small round shapes, sensitively conceived in construction and surface. By means of non-schematic movements and a unique grasp of essential characteristics, figure scenes arise naturally out of the lines and shadow reliefs assume a plastic form. These personal sketches (by this word, both method and point of view can be characterized) are marked by a certain momentariness. They are ephemeral expressions, a product of the moment, originating in the occasional activity (not constant work), mainly before winter celebrations, such as the narration of hunting tales and other experiences. This art has not yet a social character. They are really only sketches where the complexities of life are reduced to simple conceptual abstractions.

In the various objects we can thus see the common beginning of the creative adjustment of man with the world. In contrast to regular handicraft work there is sudden excitement similar to outbursts. Man with few ties in an unstable social system reacts from time to time to the impressions he has of the world surrounding him and embodies the objects of his desires in pictures and sculptures. Since he is not hampered by conceptions and since he thinks in the terms of pictures, his drawings, paintings and carvings are surprising in their unstylized truthfulness and vitality. People, who are still unable to distinguish perception from fancy and for whom the physical data merge with subjective thought, confront nature directly without associations and concepts. This then explains the directness and truthfulness of their profound visual perception, their acute sense of observation which assimilates and communicates through the drawing or carving the experiences of a life-long process of cognition. Such is the sense of observation of the hunter, a sense for the appearance and movements of the animal so sharp because on it depends his livelihood. Primitive man is so intensively taken up with the object of his interest and need that he is lost in it. And because the objective sensation corresponds to fantasy, he brings about and visualizes phenomena by means of *likenesses* created in a moment of compulsion. By pictorial likenesses the primitive mind conjures up and takes possession of the killed game, for at this stage of development the picture has the validity of reality, an authentic reality attained through the magical realization of the will. Frobenius speaks of such a mentality when he relates of an African Pigmy hunter who before sunset drew in the sand a picture of an antelope which he then shot with his arrow. Before the hunt he thus conjured up the desired prey by magic. Such hunter's magic explains the vital causes for the rise of art. Similar magic was practised in pre-historic times where too the necessities of life led to the necessity for art.

Of course, in the art of prehistoric times as well as that of primitive nations man expressed himself not only by visualizing objects by means of likeness but also by mere *symbols*. Likenesses express life as a whole whereas symbols represent only a conceptual reference. In short, it is graphical or objective shorthand sign serving as the basis for vivification and imagery where fantasy completes the suggestion of form—in the same way as a wrapped-up piece of wood becomes a doll or living being for a child. Whereas forms have a protean instability and the instantaneity of time, signs and symbols indicate a permanence and they function as analogies and indirect representations of acts. These two ways of the depiction, by likeness and symbols, are perhaps caused by the variations in psycho-physical make-up. In both cases, however, the instinct for artistic expression is given an outlet. It is this aspect of human behaviour which sublimates physical data into the terms of forms, which transforms physiological and mechanical acts into psychic ones reflecting in man the world and time.

From such beginnings, from an involuntary compulsion testified by art of primitive nations and tribes, man progressed in proportion with the development of means of production and with changing conditions. With the growth and stabilization of primitive society, mental life developed and mutual relations and relations to the world became more complicated. The religious elements together with legal principles, the moral code, etc. stabilized into a system of rites, customs and principles. At these stages of development people explained natural phenomena and experiences by the interference of supernatural forces. They surrounded themselves with demons, fantastically distorted phenomena and facts until a whole system of ideas and conceptions governed their lives, a system which is expressed in art. As the economy and organization of society developed into still broader and more complicated forms, so the nature of art changed. It is thus possible to classify the ethnic groups, from the artifacts preserved, not only geographically or into cultural spheres but also according to the stage of development. For example, as the roving collector of fruits and the hunter changed into a herdsman or settled farmer, there resulted changes in livelihood, in the attitude to nature, in the forms and aims of thinking, in purposive work as well as free creative art. It can be seen that with the stabilization of the level of material existence the conceptual elements outgrew the elements of sensual perception and super-sensual notions multiplied. These changes are revealed for example in idols, at first tersely and simply conceived, later more complicated. Some of them remain mere pieces of raw material, being only incompletely elaborated by suggestions of the head and body and general references to the limbs in crudely worked wood and stone blocks. In these idols of ancestors, of good and bad spirits, is found the first vitalizing process, the development of attempts at expressing and incarnating the sensations, intuitions and fears which pressed on man who slowly penetrated the mysteries of the unknown and incompletely mastered nature. The rough and unfinished quality of some of the works resemble mere outcries—still without the coherency of complete thoughts. Such schematic pictures were conceived without particular ingenuity—evidently in a society still in the fluid process of change which was wanting in the necessary tools but, nonetheless, required a certain inner certitude, an orientation in the world, and a correlation of objective experiences with subjective fears and feelings. There was a crude piece of raw material at first. It was a thing, that means, it was lifeless. Only by working, even in the most general way, was the feeling of life aroused. This meant the introduction of a magic content into the material, the religious embodiment of the conceptions of the ancestors. This was connected with the conception of the soul and incited this conception, awakening a sense of permanence.

Gradually the inchoate, obscure signs, visible in various parts of the world, acquired plastic form and distinctness. The simple block-like sculptures of ancestors were further developed by the articulation of individual parts. The shaping of idols became a craft. The crafts then maintained the tradition by repetition and familiarization with the material. If the original signs and symbols still sought to mimic the innuendos of life—by carving sharp edges, the addition of parts to serve as limbs, by profiles or simple colouring and costumes—the material later came to be regarded as something passive to be worked upon and perfected by *technique* which is nothing more than skill acquired through the repetition of certain acts. In repeated acts man acquaints himself with the material, recognizes its intrinsic properties, and endeavours to conform to its peculiarities through appropriate methods of treatment, deliberately enlivening it with expression.

Artistic expression is motion, physical and spiritual, extending into the realm of fantasy. Sometimes it proceeds completely from the inside of man, at other times reflects the surrounding world, but it is always manifested in rhythm which has the ability to bind, to contemplate, characterize, analyse, synthetize, abstract and value. We know that rhythm wells forth in man most spontaneously in moments of heightened existence and tension, intoxication or rapture. It is latently present in the living functions of the body and comes to the fore in dance and music in which man transcends through his rhythmic motion and whirling the mundane world into an ecstatic state, such as is the case with ritual dancers and sorcerers of various nations and tribes. The rhythmic motion and music, and also the decoration and mask, transports them during rituals and magic acts into a state of heightened tension, they "change" into the gods whose likeness they have adopted, "arise" from the earthly world into another, higher world of the gods. In many cases in these dances with masks there crystallizes not only a mass ecstasy but a *common conception of the other world*. In this conception there merge superstitions, witchcraft, memories of dead ancestors, belief in demons dwelling in nature, conviction of an after-life and the transmigration of the soul, notions on the origin of sickness and its treatment and even the principles of social organization. At a certain stage of development this conception completely reigns over the fundamental material life, determines the main components of cultural superstructure and forms in the life of the society a common *content* which is then made manifest through art.

At this stage creative activity goes beyond a mere mechanical conception of the world, vitalizes nature with good and evil spirits that abound in the trees, wells, rocks, animals, mountains, thunder and lightning. This other world, created in conceptions, is an organic continuation of the external world. Although invisible, it nevertheless profoundly affects life and death, society and the progress of time. It dictates the social institutions, altars, temples and burial grounds; it defines the relationship towards nature and adds colour to existential necessity. Thus there emerges a basic conception of life with definite notions on its good and bad aspects. Should the economic base be broad enough, this crude philosophy becomes embodied in *style*. Here human relations represented by forms play a counterpoint to nature. Needless to say, such a unity does not spring from æsthetic design but simply from organic life itself, filled with purposive labour and time.

Superstructure of this kind is repeatedly seen in *Africa*, where several cultures of varying levels of development came into existence in conformity with definite economic and social systems. The evolution of ancestor worship, which was initially engendered by a fear of the spirit of the dead and the veneration of gods residing in objects, plants, and animals, crystallized the original superstitions and witchcraft into religious systems, organizations and unions. The crafts which were practised regularly by the more gifted tribes conventionalized the idols of ancestors, demons and fetishes in the form of tools, decorations, and pure art works, all of which were closely bound by a rigid tradition. Style is here the composite result of the fusion of the subject with life, material, technique and function. The forms are the representations of man's inherent instincts and impulses and serve at the same time as remembrances, charms and symbols. In them the common fear is permanently recorded. They are the direct outgrowth of ceremony, they express man's conceptions of relations, the conclusions of his pre-logical thinking and a consciousness of the system of consanguinity. In them is formulated *totemism*, a conception born of life's experiences and the feeling of helplessness against nature, embodied in the system of family ties. The belief in the kinship with animals certainly contributed towards the birth of the nation of spirits personified in symbols and totem signs. In the same manner *fetishism*, arising out of ancestor worship, led to the incarnation of spirits in the idols. Thereby a world is created in which man is surrounded by the mysteries of the elements, of life and death. The conceptions of this world have been consistently and uniformly condensed in works of art expressing the inherent bonds of a certain circle in the system of forms. In Negro art this system of forms includes burial sculptures, idols of demons and ancestors, masks, thrones, tools, jewels, and sceptres—free art next to utilitarian objects. The first artistic motives mingle here with the results of a later development. The long bodies and large heads give the impression of tranquillity and massiveness, for motion is carried through in one direction only and abruptly terminated. The basic feature is permanence. It is proclaimed in the concentration of volume and the emphasis of ethnic types, the raising of the profiles of the eyebrows and mouth so that the expression is compact, in harmony with the content, form and function. Both the large and small works simplify and exaggerate the body markings, outline, volume, and apertures without regard to natural proportions. The craftsman worked toward a coherent flow of rounded surfaces and towards an imposing spread in space defined by the base from which the frontal bodies project. The bodies are consistent in plastic transposition, even in relief decorations indicating tattooing on the body. The sculptures themselves allude to countless situations but always the same attitude to life. They are capable of expressing motherhood and other concepts quite accurately although the conventional form conceals the personal creative individuality. Even if we may be unfamiliar with the significance of a certain object and its content may be strange to us, we can nevertheless sense the forceful expressiveness of thinking which is otherwise incommunicable; we can perceive the fancies of exotic cults and the power of life translated to cubic forms beyond the measure of time and the environment in which they arose.

An elementary conviction in the existence of another world apart from visible reality led in *Africa* to the creation of masks and decoration. The heightened consciousness leads to an ecstatic outburst and rapture expressed in the dance with masks which transform the wearer, establish new relations and impart the power to alter the normal order of things. Rhythm takes the place of logic not only in the content of these dances but also in the shape of the masks which simplify and abstract new signs and reduce the original image of the skull by abbreviations. Whether they be masks of secret societies or religious paraphernalia used in initiation ceremonies, the anatomical features of the head are reduced to mere suggestions of the eyes, nose, mouth and hair which the rhythm now takes up, develops and transforms into fearful phantoms. In this way man escapes from his own conception of natural laws.

In the art collections from various nations, countries and historical periods, the intense monumentality of African art inevitably stands out in striking contrast to the works of *Oceania*. The contrast is seen in their disharmony and tendency to destroy the natural texture of the material by means of wholly ornamental workmanship. Of course, notable variations are to be met with depending on the ethnic type and stage of economic development: from crude products still groping for form to complex and intricate art in Borneo, the Philippines, New Guinea and Sumatra. Next to vague witchcraft we find complicated religious cults. The influences of by-gone times and intercourse with neighbouring cultures have also left their mark.

Everywhere, in the simple as well as complex forms we find man, his relationship to nature and society, various secret ceremonials, his belief in ghosts and phantoms, protecting spirits and ancestors. In *Australia* the burial stones are simple markings, a rough piece of material imparted with edges, flat surface and point. Similarly, elaborate figures of ancestors and chieftains do not exist among the *Bataks* of Sumatra, the *Dajaks* of Borneo or even among the *Hawaiians*. From the feeble Australian ornaments which are confined to purely elementary forms we may go on and follow the manner in which man endowed life to matter as, for example, in *New Caledonia* where we come across striving for body movements, expression of the head and somatic types. On the island of *Nias* this is represented by plain, angular, at times crudely profiled blocks of wood with a large head. At other times the wood is profiled or hollowed, with edges and surfaces, or the projecting ends add life to the material and transform it, with more or less extensive treatment, into the bearer of beliefs and desires. But just as in *Sepik*, the structural perpendiculars, fortifications and geometric notchings in Nias frequently lose the natural texture of the material as a result of the excessive globularity in the sculpturing. This discloses a groping attempt to express the vitality of the body and a fondness for new forms.

XVI

The rendering of an object life-like through differentiation of the principal parts of the body into head, neck, trunk and legs, is never complete in Oceania. The material remains unchanged and a life-like unity is not always attained. The African art works are much more consistent in their interpretation of life, more complete and active in a plastic sense. In the Philippines and on the Solomon Islands, in fact on all islands, we encounter huge idols that are distorted into fear-evoking images. Usually they are unstable in their positions, and even the larger figures often do not stand firmly. Not only the dance figures of the Baining-Ahreigs on *New Pomerania*, which reach 35 to 40 metres in height and are made of specially processed and painted bark, but even the colossal stone statues on *Easter Island* are not conceived from a thorough plastic point of view. The flatness of the head which is worked out spatially blends imperceptibly with the roundness of the stone; the object has no organic unity but remains only a suggestion. Only where exact craftmanship was maintained did tradition lead to a systematic elaboration of the details into a unified whole. Harmonious organic forms appeared only when the material made the rendition of the theme in an imposing expression possible. This came about by way of a methodical *ornamentation* which developed the feelings and imaginations through abbreviations, eliminations, combinations and the logical use of old and new forms. Here as elsewhere we observe that for a craftsman who is intimately in contact with nature and is guided by a purpose in life does not exist such a thing as valueless material, the question of taste does not arise. Aside from turtle shells and pearls, wood is utilized simultaneously with bird feathers and grass which lend an astonishing harmony and fantastic expressiveness to the ceremonial costumes, utilitarian objects and works of pure art. The result of this application of ornament is the common feature of detachment from life, an emphasis on the super-real whereby man is cut loose from nature.

Sometimes, as in the case of the *Maoris* in *New Zealand*, rhythm of ornamentation acts in the following manner: the structure of the object is hidden under a rhythmical whirlpool of lines, which refines it into an ornament and goes beyond it. With the *Dayaks* and *Bataks*, too, the ornament places the components in a quite unexpected correlation, unknown to our causal-logical conceptions, and develops the mythological details into a highly involved fantasy so that there appears an independent whole governed by its own logic and laws of growth which is realized not so much by composition as by the addition of parts. The flat reduction of the plastic elements, the division of accents and coupling of parts according to the sense of the shapes, the new combinations or distortions, remove the subject matter into another category and establish mystic relations.

The ornamentative character is effectively augmented by *colouring* which in *Oceania* often replaces sculpturing. Primitive man never leaves a surface bare but inevitably covers it with colour, contrasts which even more increase the unnaturalness and ornamental correlation of the details and multiply the symbolic elements. The complicated design on the utilitarian and ceremonial objects is unintelligible to the outside observer. But a member of the particular cultural community is immediately able to understand from the coloured ornament the involved message expressed in this rhythmical movement which becomes a base-line for the tribal community and tribal psychology. The consistency of this art has meaning, however, even to the outsider; even he senses the importance of the conclusions of this so-called pre-logical thinking which arises from other connections than strictly causal; even he feels the secrets and fears embodied in the works.

This fear and cruelty is best expressed in cannibal *Melanesia*, in the carvings similar to thin scaffolding, cut out from the outside to the inside and dematerialized by the vivid painting. Symbols of *toucan*, the bird of death, snakes and dead ancestors exert a profound influence on the life of the living. Tall pierced reliefs, divided into curves, notches and profiles help to disclose the potentialities of the material and give it symbolic significance. The expressive quality of motion seems sometimes like a terrible dream, it conveys a sort of inner amazement and gives a different meaning to life and death. It represents an intimate symbolism which in Melanesia is carried out with consistency by the logic of art and the certitude of idea which leaves its impress on the structure and makes of it the bearer of ideas by means of sculptural and colour decorations. The rhythmic play of ornament and colour intermingles with a continual reminder of death and horror.

If we follow the art production of various countries and regions, we discover that by and large it does not depict the period and its people but is their product and reflection, often very far from reality. In spite of it it is possible to discern in the art forms the mutual ties of the members of a certain society, how they looked upon and regarded nature, what they thought and felt. From the art expressions extant in the different countries of *South America*, we can reconstruct the inter-relationships of its inhabitants before the discovery and conquest by the Europeans. Written records speak of nations which resided in the mountains and plains of Cordillera. They comprised several nations, but the civilization they created is related and sequential. The *Mayas* were evidently much older than the *Aztecs*. Some of their artifacts in South Mexico and Yucatan may perhaps exhibit a certain non-schematicism and vitality. On the whole, however, the individual works of pre-Columbian America are united by a peculiar complexity and abstractness, a heavy fullness and frequent portrayal of monsters; the passion for dealing with murders and human sacrifices is a morbid reflection of sun worship. The architecture, sculptures and paintings form a system the complexity of which corresponds to a highly developed economic and social system, rigid administrative bureaucracy, class hierarchy and state military organization. This can be detected in the ornate figures of demons that lie submerged among the profuse reliefs on the magnificent ruins of pyramids and temples: the moaning naked spirit of man, perplexed and trembling, cast without protection into an evil world. The dimensions are super-human, indeed, non-human. We feel the ceremonial cannibalism and the blood dripping from the bodies and ornaments bound by a firm system which represent certain concepts and religious codes. Both the large and small works are done without particular regard for the qualities of the material; both the stones and fired clay are rigid and stiff and their stiffness serves to intensify the impression of phantasmagory in human sacrifices. It is an incredible art in which everything human is transformed into an abstraction that ignores proportion, in which the living becomes a schematic image through a reduction of form and shape—leaving only the elementary, strangely powerful expression of sadness, pain and horror.

The point of departure for the patternization of this art was evidently the advancements of stylization of fabrics. It resulted in a quality of flatness which contrasted to the potter's workmanship. The fusion of techniques explains the jaggedness, exaggeration and linear quality of the ornaments which were placed on the precisely symmetrical figures. As a general rule, the aim was to make an abstraction of the body type, movements and expression, which is terse and at times out of harmony in the independent details.

The extensiveness, formal consistency and conceptual schematization of the pre-Columbian American cultures now and then remind one of ancient Egypt—equally super-human. The invasion of the Spaniards interrupted the line of development so that only certain features show the continuity of definite ideas and concepts in the tools and decorations of the *South American Indians*. An example of this are the bomb-like vessels which are only worked out slightly and loosely covered with painted decorations. Even more feeble are the tools and geometric ornaments done on fabrics by the inhabitants of Tierra del Fuego and the tribes of southern-most America.

The division of the American continent is manifest also in the superstructure of the *Northern* and *Northwestern Indians*, economically and culturally a more firmly-knit community. It is expressed in the well-developed art crafts and the uniformity of symbolic signs for concepts and relations which are developed in a rich pictorial language. It is not simply a pictorial system of writing—epic in scope—but a complex representation of the totem structure of society as conveyed in the masks, figures of animals, and unified conception of the humanized motifs taken from nature. The high standard of living is shown by the energetic profiles and contrasting colours, rich variations of the eye motif, and precise pottery work which is delineated cleanly and in which the ornament is always secondary to function, never extending beyond a certain point. The relationship of individual forms with the pre-Columbian period may be demonstrated in the manner of abbreviations, idea-content, reduction of volume, a sardonic hardness, and suggestions of anger and pain in some of the masks. The logic of the art set these totem-poles against nature, symbolizing the temporal succession of ancestors in terms of artistic verticality. The tree trunks were opened up vigorously with large and oblique profiles and holes without destroying the flow and continuity of the material. The original texture of the wood was covered with colours to indicate the eyes, nose, beak, mouth and claws. Likenesses of tribal animals merge with human likenesses.

This introduction, dealing with the enormous art production scattered all over the world, naturally notes only the formal logic and general features of the individual areas. But even such superficial observation immediately discloses certain social and intrinsic characteristics of this art. First of all, the differences in the relationship toward nature and within individual social groupings are striking. The degree and character of social development is seen. Art transcends the bounds of time, contracts the distance between epochs and peoples, and reverts man back to the primordial stage of cognition, animation, expression and creation. At the same time it shows the basic direction in which ethnic groups are moving: systems erected on super-stitions, sexual necessities, practical activity, customs codified in laws, dreams, poems, incomplete knowledge and feelings are melted in moulds of styles. Thus the most powerful factor in life, time, becomes tangible, for creative work is a process of continual re-encounter with the past and an incessant struggle with the ever-changing present. The new stands next to the old, the primitive next to the sophisticated culture. The creative process makes the artist to manifest himself and the humanity.

The uninterrupted flow of time is especially evident in the art of ancient *Egypt*. As in the case of pre-Columbian America, it is possible to trace in Egyptian art the conservatism of style in a rigid state and religious system. In the early Egyptian works there are evidences of the transition from sporadic volatile expressiveness of primitive art to the stylistic code of civilization. Hypothetically at least, it is possible to re-construct the connection between the drawings of the bushmen, which are isolated forms, improvisations and sketches, with the pictures of animals left behind by the early Egyptian artists. The sketchy vagueness of the paintings gradually changed into hieroglyphic ideograms and led to a strictly defined system of narration and conceptions. The common bond of rhythm and craft repetition of acts acted on this system so that the individual personal forms acquired a common idea-content; the individual changed into a general symbol and finally reflected a generally accepted social form. Types were created through co-operation and visual sketches assumed another meaning.

In the beginning of Egyptian art there were drawings, engraved and embossed lines, delicate and precise, which provided the outline. Work with stone increased their coherency and distinctness. Primitive conceptions merged into new forms to give rise to new shapes and thus to a definitive realization of a certain aspect, division of parts, stylisation and unity of the whole. Soon, the sculptures became harsh in quality, compact in volume, smooth on the surface and graphic in stylization. Lines, symmetrical arrangements, weight and flatness are multiplied in the sculptures. The paintings and statues have little plasticity, the starting point being clearly relief lines, edges and flat surfaces. The lifeless historified form then persists in essential masses both in the large and small figures; they are immobile and penetrate into space only by means of their limbs. Even the bronzes are like stones, being conceived in flat reliefs; only occasionally is there a more determined effort to expand the system and to enrich the outlines of the figures which are realized in block forms, arranged symmetrically and usually developed in the front and back but never on all sides. The attempt at realism is limited to details, whereas the general conception and composition retain the symbolism of the stylistic canon and the idea-content.

As an outstanding characteristics the art of various countries of *Asia Minor* exhibits likewise a comprehension of art-forms in terms of reliefs, lending itself thereby to an emphasis of the side view. A layout in horizontal zones and a linear quality predominate. In contrast to the Egyptian stone, the most important medium was clay, which was substantially unchanged and was only decorated on the surface with subtle treatment. Neither did artistically shading glyptics interfere with the organism of things but only the colour of the glaze was used to increase the effect of the surfaces. The massive and relatively short bodies appear to be without skeleton and coherency; the ornamental character of the art is shown by the profusion of isolated details and the abundant use of ornaments which were evidently derived from fabrics. Textiles influenced even the configuration of the figures, the heavy disposition of the legs, and the inexpressible grandeur of the narrated scenes which in Assyria and Babylonia are sometimes arranged in an amazingly colourful architectonic whole.

A historical analysis of art solves the questions of inter-dependence of development, follows the changes and influences of time, and traces the evolution of motifs through various lands and ages. Moreover, it also deals with phenomena that are general and unique for art and its effect on the life of peoples. In entering the world created by the Asian craftsmen and artists in the course of centuries, we become aware of the fact that eastern art is based on a totally different *conception of time*, that it differs from European art above all in its duration and serenity of being, in distinct contrast to the turbulence and constant changes in Europe. Another phenomenon in Asian art worthy of consideration is rusticalization, the process wherein the extraneous frills of content and form are amalgamated from one sphere or class into another. The foreign form is copied in this process and is only incompletely introduced into a new surrounding—be it class or nation—which only partially understands and assimilates the style. Rusticalization does not necessarily mean schematization, flattening, or deadening; often such imitation and assimilation give birth to new æsthetic values and establish new codes. In the incomplete imitation of the style a new content makes its appearance which the prototypes did not have. Another important part played by Asian art is its share in the formulation of religious thoughts and social principles. It is a culture-forming factor, a power which makes the fluid social life crystallize into nations and distinct ethnic individuality. We find such to be the case in the art of India, Central and East Asia, especially when following the geographic and temporal progress of Buddhist art.

Buddhism came into being in India, in a territory separated from the rest of Asia by mountains. It was in these mountains that various religious theories were born. Their philosophical content, a pantheistic allegorization of natural forces, was expounded by an involved pictorial language utilizing epic style and elaborating body signs in fantastic ornamental design. Typical of the religious art of India is the allegoric interpretation of the idea of unity of man with the universe and the idea of the cycle of life and death. Their interpretations often led to new combinations of forms according to written texts and legends. The basic tranquillity is in no way depreciated by the completeness of subordination and the ornate workmanship done by special artisans. Because the art works originated in repetition and the requirements of ritual ceremony which dictated the body positions, proportioning and compositions, it can be said that they were made rather than created. They led to magnificent conventions corresponding to the ceremonies, principles and illustrations of cosmic processes.

The philosophical teachings of Buddhism regard the external world as a veil and a dream. As elsewhere, the thoughts and philosophical conceptions evolved into artistically transposed symbolic conceptions which made of this most philosophical religion a legend centering around the figure of Buddha. At some point shortly before or after the birth of Christ, Europe made its contribution to the creation of Buddhist art through the influence of its Hellenistic sculptures which were introduced in the Greek kingdoms of present-day Afghanistan, Turkistan and in *Gandhara* in North-West India. The result was a rustication of the Greek non-symbolic love of the body and vitality. In the figure of Buddha, the Apollonic type became an ideal divine being as a result of the rhythmic elaboration of the drapery, symmetrical frontal design and harmony of the ornamental and body elements. The Gandhara Buddha in stone and stucco lost the three-dimensional quality and became rigid by the use of linear elements, but with the emergence of a new idea-content it acquired a further quality, namely, serenity. The centuries of thought and feeling of Indian religious teaching graphically reveal a yearning for perfection, a wise dispassionateness and inner certitude. Buddha standing and conferring blessings, Buddha seated on a lotus throne in a ritual pose of penitence,—this was the personification of a religion which negated the world and each act and link with the outside world. The pose, which had a basis in definite ideas, and the gestures were not without consequences in the arrangement of the axes, centre of gravity, linear design and disposition in space. The painstaking craftsmanship further advanced the expression of serenity and quietude by means of forms which matured in the course of centuries until each globularity, markings of the hair, and prescribed body signs gained a new firm plasticity. Time developed the idea which in turn acted on the religious system regardless of the particular country in question and regardless of the amalgamation it underwent with the vestiges of ancient indigenous beliefs and conceptions.

Buddhist conceptions also had effect in those places where the original purity of asceticism was not strictly adhered to, that is to say, in Lamaist *Tibet*, where its principles were intermingled not only with Indian tantristic ritual but also with indigenous witchcraft. Around Buddha there arose the complicated Lamaist pantheon personifying cosmic principles and natural forces with horrible gods and demons. A ponderous exuberance which, however, does not minimize the clarity, hieratic serenity and impassiveness of certitude proclaims the transcendentalism of this cosmology in the firm outlines of the Lamaistic and Nepalese bronzes. The movements of the whole and of the parts resembles stone, as the basis which continues in the smooth bronze forms and the ornamental decoration of details. In the paintings there are ceremonial codes, logic and stylistic purity so that even in a small measure they take on the monumental unity of surface, form, colour and idea.

Through trade routes from India across Central Asia, the figure of Buddha came to *China* where it enriched the wisdom based on an astronomic conception of the world and crystallized in a definite social code. The great harmony of earth and heaven was reflected not only in the teachings of Taoism and Confucius but also, in its own way, in the tools, architecture, painting and sculpture. There was a definite system even in Chinese Buddhist expressions; the crafts fused with art and personal experiences with stylistic conventions. In each piece of art-work there is something of a great music, just as there is logic in the fantasy and creation of symbols. The symbol of the dragon, phoenix and other legendary forms in the Chinese formulation took on a singular unity and effectiveness, one might say a certain naturalness. The monsters, elaborated in perfect coherence of real and imagined elements, received a new reason for being. Painting, like sculpture, was an account of life, a knowledge of the world and an interpretation of the world order as measured by time and the senses. The fine craftsmanship which produced the exquisite curve of the neck and belly of ceramic vases, was also applied in the finer arts, in the personal artistic expressions which grew from style above style.

The profound concentration and experiencing of time and world, which we admire in Chinese poetry, is found even in the painting, which in its fundamental idea-content achieves a truthfulness and melodic tone. It is not composed of piece meal design, it is not a description. It flows naturally as an extension of experience, out of a sense for unity and comprehension of composition. The synthetic lines freely set the forms on a flat surface and transpose the manifoldness of nature into concentrated images which have character, meaning and value. Consequently, from the basis in life and craftsmanship there emerged in China distinct art characteristics which constantly grew through the heritage of the past.

Chinese art is the amazing world of forms made logical through a unity of form and content and naturally bridging the gap between fine and applied arts. *Japanese art* inherited something of the great spirit of China.

The strength of the Japanese lies in an intelligent perception and higher decree of workmanship. Of course even with this elegance and technical brilliancy in art that was purposely decorative, we find that the small and large works have a certain truthfulness. A shrewdly perceived and interpreted reality is brought to a common denominator of style. In the work there is a fusion of a definite idea-content and a theme with a purpose; the subjective content is united with a common belief and is made objective by the advancements of multiple tradition. Here art serves the philosophy of life and social laws.

We have seen that this is true everywhere. We outsiders appreciate the formal aspects of art, the breadth and depth of style, and the vitality of expression. In doing so, however, we miss, on the whole, that which lies beneath the form: the concrete needs, teachings, purposes. But nevertheless we realize that the vital expressiveness of the art ot the nations of various countries and regions flowed from the fact that creative work was only a continuation of labour and necessary expressions of life and never special traits gained at the margin of social life. Beauty and personality were only the side products of an attempt to fulfil a definite aim.

Beauty, just as truth, good and love, does not exist a priori outside of man. It is created by man in the course of his life and encounter with the world which he knows, uses and evaluates. Therefore, contemporary art, too, requires a basis in real life, if art expression is not to become sterile and empty. It must be continually nurtured by humanism. It is this very humanism which we find in the art of distant lands, distant from us in ways and thoughts. The conception and workmanship are often foreign to us and yet the creator of these works is familiar to us through his effort to bring order, formulate, express himself and give voice to the meaning of life. Through this common content the distant countries and by-gone times become comprehensible to us because in them we come to know people, very human, and learn to understand man's eternal struggle with matter. Consequently, we find the present even in the world of remote forms.

V. V. Štech

Egypt

AKHNATON AND THE AMARNA PERIOD

Our modest collections of the artistic works of ancient Egypt do not permit us to trace the whole development of ancient Egyptian art, even less so as the works chosen have been taken for the most part from private collections. Even for a short explanation, if this is not to be incomplete, examples must be chosen from among works scattered throughout many museums all over the world. This publication has another aim: to acquaint its reader with objects which would otherwise remain for a long time inaccessible to the general public. Thus the reader must resort to other, more detailed books on Egyptian art. Before going on to discuss our subject proper which concerns one of the most interesting sculptures of our private collections, we will therefore give only a general explanation and brief chronological survey of the most important stages in the art of one of the oldest cultures of mankind.

The first typical expressions of Egyptian art come from the prehistoric period which, in the region of the Nile Valley, came to a close about 3000 B. C. In addition to the drawings on rocks and vessels this particularly concerns magnificent ceramics. Reliefs in stone, already bearing the marks of Egyptian art, appear towards the end of this period, shown by a number of outstanding examples. At the beginning of the historical period the Egyptians already excelled for the perfection of their jewellery. Further development and at the same time the first great point of culmination was reached in architecture, sculpture and painting in the period of the centralized state during the 3rd to 6th dynasties (period of the Old Kingdom, about 2800-2300 B. C.). The realistic statues, reliefs and mural pictures showing scenes from the life of that time, were for many years the pattern and basis for art of the later periods. Egyptian art developed further about 2000 B. C. during the period of the formation of the new era in the history of Egypt, the so-called Middle Kingdom, and particularly during the 11th and 12th dynasties. With liberation from the Hyksos rule and the foundation of a new and powerful state after 1500 B. C., when Egypt became a world power, the old heritage won fresh appreciation; the reliefs, statues and mural pictures reached their peak in the fineness of their works and elegance replaced robustness (New Kingdom, particularly 18th and 19th dynasties). The Amarna period under a king of the 18th dynasty, Akhnaton, was outstanding for its reaction to a number of stylistic expressions in art and a return to healthy realism. Later, when Egyptian power declined under the impact of the struggle for liberation by the subject countries and the formation of strong states in Asia, Egyptian art still flourished in what is known as the Late Period (after 1000 B. C.), particularly during the Saite (26th) dynasty (663-525) as a result of further expansion of the Old Kingdom art. The art of ancient Egypt was not without influence on the classical art of Greece and Rome; on the other hand, Greek influence on Egyptian art was greater only during the Ptolemaic period (from 322 B. C.). Less important is the Coptic art (art of the Egyptian Christians) which even after the occupation of Egypt by the Arabs in 640 A. D. still drew on native themes. Gradually, however, with the dissolution of the economic order of ancient Egypt, art was based less and less on the tradition which had preserved its typical features and the Egyptians, losing their original language and religion, came under the direct influence of Arab life and art.

A study of the culture of ancient Egypt, however, continually presents new opportunities for a more correct judgment of the evolution of the whole of mankind. The favourable climatic conditions in Egypt preserved for us cultural relics in such abundance and from materials which elsewhere would have rotted long since, that it is possible to form a picture of nearly five thousand years of uninterrupted cultural development of this country. This shows us the causal connection, an explanation of which is easy here, whereas in other regions similar cases are subject to many hypotheses and theories, often quite erroneous. In determining the development of art the unique example of ancient Egypt shows us how incorrect were the opinions of art historians who judged the artistic creations of human hands without simultaneously studying the economic and social conditions of society in which the creators of these works of art lived and worked. For this reason every contribution to a knowledge of such conditions is valuable in studying the corresponding epochs in the development of art. This is all the more true of such a turbulent time in the history of ancient Egypt as was the period of the Akhnaton reforms in the spheres of religion and art—a period so often interpreted incorrectly.

Few personalities in ancient Egyptian history have aroused such wide-spread interest as this "enraptured dreamer," this "exalted fanatic," "heretic king," "reformer and revolutionary pharaoh," "doctrinarian pacifist," "the most fascinating personality which ever sat on the throne of the pharaohs" and "one of the most amazing figures in the history of mankind," the tenth ruler in the 18th dynasty—Amenhotep IV-Akhnaton.

Writers in the Greek language have scarcely preserved for us his name; Egyptian tradition itself had evaded the issue, even avoiding the use of his name, referring to Akhnaton as "the enemy of Akhetaton" and speaking of his reign as "the years of the Rebel." Modern research, depending on a knowledge of the ancient Egyptian and Babylonian languages (state archives were discovered in Amarna where the correspondence with Asia was written in the Babylonian language) and a profound study of material relics, have gradually penetrated the veil of oblivion which has shrouded this figure of ancient times and, as though desiring to make up for the long years of silence, Akhnaton has become one of the most famous individuals in the history of ancient Egypt.

Akhnaton has not always been interpreted correctly, even by experts in Egyptian history. We are not surprised therefore to find the novelists' accounts even more dubious when they have taken up this figure with such enthusiasm. But even many historians have divorced Akhnaton from any relationship to the times in which he lived and have paid no attention to some important conditions which did not seem to them to be in direct relationship to the king as a reformer.

First it is completely incorrect to see the reason for Akhnaton's acts in his own individuality (one historian, for example, puts forth the utterly baseless contention that Akhnaton was not a pure-blooded Egyptian, while according to another, whose theory is similarly without proof, he was ill, while still others claim that Akhnaton was influenced by his wife's Asiatic origin, a supposition which is in itself extremely doubtful). Similarly, it is erroneous to concentrate on his religious reforms and see their reason in the statesman's attempt to give the Egyptian empire of his day a world religion, not only a narrow national one. It would be equally wrong, on the other hand, to rule out wholly the king's individual part in such many-sided reforms. It is enough to recall that the hatred of later ages was turned almost exclusively against the person of Akhnaton and not to any such degree against his reforms and that the king was not supported in his innovations either by any single broad segment of the ruling class or by the mass of the people.

About 1580 B. C., the Egyptians, under the leadership of the Upper Egyptian king, Ahmose, who was living in the city of Weset (later Thebes in Greco-Roman times) succeeded in driving the Asiatic occupants, the Hyksos, from their land. This marked a new era in Egyptian history, the period of the New Kingdom with the 18th dynasty at its head. The centre of resistance and only hope for independence for the Egyptians was Weset where even in the preceding dynasty the kings had struggled for independence. After the victory, Weset became the most important city in all Egypt and soon overshadowed the capital, Mennofer (later Memphis of the Greeks), in its size and splendour. The patron god of Weset, Amon, who in the eyes of the nation helped the Egyptians in their victory, was elevated to king of the gods and identified with the most important deities.

The successors of Ahmose were educated in the tradition of the fight of both the Weset dynasties against the Asiatics. The recent subjugation of their country and the history of the past centuries had taught them that at a time when Asia was seething with migration of nations and forming more and more powerful states it was not enough to depend upon the defences with which the early dynasties of the Middle Kingdom had protected themselves against raids by Asiatic tribes into the fertile Nile Valley, namely, internal peace, a strong central government and strong fortifications along the Egyptian-Asian border.

Such were the lessons learned from the destruction of the Old Kingdom and used by the Middle Kingdom; the insurrection of the

5

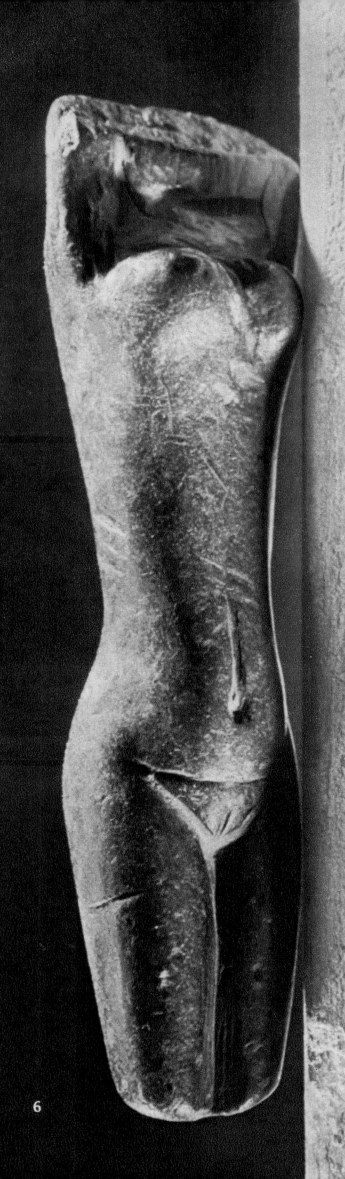

Hyksos equipped with military horse-drawn chariots, the compound bow, and bronze and iron weapons, testified to the new situation pertaining in Asia and showed that new measures were necessary. The New Kingdom found those new measurements in enrolling foreign mercenaries in their army, in perfecting their military technique following the example of the Hyksos and moving the Egyptian frontiers towards Asia and setting up buffer states under Egyptian military control. The danger of invasion from Asia was practically ruled out so long as there was peace and a strong army inside Egypt. This was the Egyptian military policy at the outset of the 18th dynasty. It would be an error to assume, however, that the kings of Egypt left it at that. From the frontier territories easy profits flowed in the form of taxes on the subject peoples, cheap labour (slaves), booty from bigger insurrections and in addition to new and hitherto unknown products from subject countries came news of even greater riches beyond the frontiers of the Egyptian protectorates. In addition, this was undoubtedly accompanied by intrigues among the different Asiatic princes who counted, in the case of necessity, on the help of a powerful neighbour against a still more disagreeable one.

So the original defensive wars and defence measures which were intended only to protect the fruits of victory, won with such difficulty, became predatory wars. These wars, in turn, were facilitated by well-trained and experienced troops under the command of the energetic kings, Thutmose I-III and Amenhotep II, who did everything to live up to the tradition of their divine origin and even more increase the glory of their "father, Amenre, conqueror of Asiatics." (Amenre is the name of Amon after his merger with the King of the Sun, Re, hence Amenre. By the close connection of the two words, the accent, in the Egyptian language, is moved and the formerly accented vowel is changed. Thus the name Re is changed to Ra—in the compound name Rameses, the Greek form of which is Ramses, etc.)

Economic prosperity brought with it a boom in culture and art. An especially high level was attained in architecture, sculpture, artistic handicrafts and literature. A real idea of the flowering of Egypt of that time can be had from the large-scale building of temples in Weset which is on the site of today's Luxor and Karnak. The kings of Weset glorified their formerly insignificant local god by vesting his temples and priests with enormous economic power. To whom else belonged rewards in the form of a rich part of the booty when the kings marched from victory to victory "thanks to Amon?"

But the kings, intoxicated with power, while considering themselves to be the living incarnations of the god Hor and sons of Re, forgot that they had made Amenre King of the Gods. The priests of Amon did not forget it, however. The High Priest of Amon held the huge economic power of the temples in his hands. Temple officials became state employees and the High Priest appropriated for himself one by one the most important state functions. Soon he became the most powerful man in Egypt after the king. The time for him to usurp the government of all Egypt and take upon himself the crown was not yet ripe. This happened after the end of the New Kingdom.

However, already Thutmose IV, the grandfather of Akhnaton, realized the danger which stemmed from the concentration of power in the hands of the representative of priests. Despite the habits of his predecessors, Thutmose awarded the post of president of the council of high priests representing all cults, not to the powerful High Priest of Amon but to a court dignitary who had formerly been an army official.

Thutmose IV ruled only 20 years, most of which were peaceful. A simple tour of the conquered countries at the outset of his reign was enough to put down any little uprising aiming at exploiting the change on the Egyptian throne. A single expedition to Nubia in the eighth year of his reign was also enough to ensure the continuation of Egyptian sovereignty in this region. Peace with Asia was ensured by Thutmose IV by friendship with the empire of Mitanni, a friendship deepened still more when he married a Mitanni princess who became a member of the Egyptian king's harem.

The father of Akhnaton, Amenhotep III, also did not act in concert with the wishes of Amon's priests who were eager for booty. This king showed, during the first years of his reign, that he was as good a military commander as his forefathers; he penetrated the furthest into Nubia. He did not make war with Asia, continuing the peace treaty his father had made with Mitanni and even sealing it by more marriages. That meant no new booty for Amon's temples.

It is true that the priests continued to receive a large share of the taxes coming from Asia and that the king was building magnificent temples to Amon. However, in spite of all this wealth one can imagine that new expansions would have been more agreeable for the priesthood. All the more so since the ruler of the powerful empire often manifested towards Amon's priests unpleasant expressions of his individual despotism. He did not disguise the fact that his wife was not of royal birth with any myths of divine intervention of Amon as was done in such cases by his predecessors. He emphasized too much his own divine substance and he also permitted temples to be sanctified to his queen as to a goddess. At the same time, he fostered too friendly relations with the priesthood of the god Re in the Upper Egyptian city of On (later Hermonthis), finally even stripping the High Priest of Amon of his position as eldest priest and giving it to a royal prince, as the Mennofer High Priest of the god Ptah. In

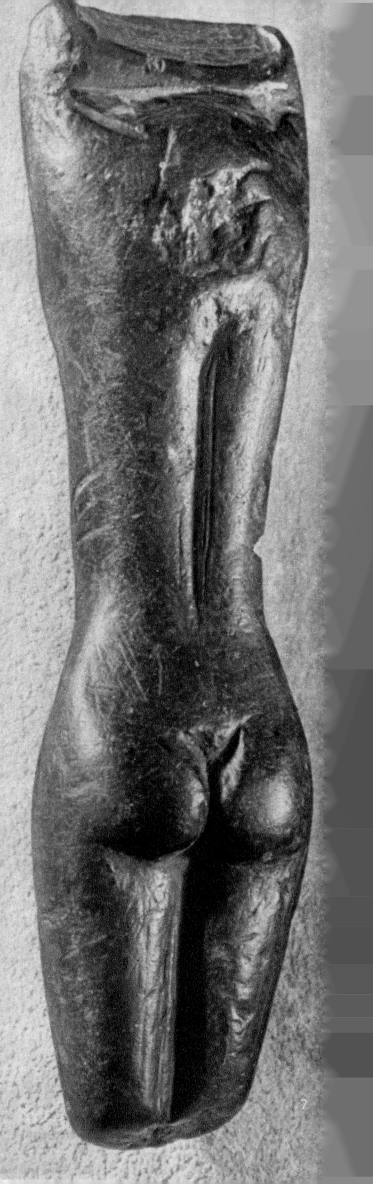

general, he supported the priesthood of the original independent cults of the sun-worshippers who did not join the cult of Amon. In addition to the Cults of the Rising Sun, Kherpri, of the Noon-day Sun, Re, and of the Setting Sun, Atum, there was also the Cult of the Sun sphere itself, Aton. (This confirms the opinion of Prof. Lexa that it was not a disc, as has always been contended, but a sun *sphere;* this follows from a comparison, made by the Egyptians themselves, between the sun and a beetle's ball, and from some Egyptian paintings. It is sufficient to consult the photograph of a piece of jewellery published in the *Journal of Egyptian Archeology*, 22, pl. XXII, fig. 4. For technical reasons, the Egyptians usually represented the sun as a disc although it is certain that they conceived it in a spherical form.)

The common word, *aton*, which means the sun's sphere, the material sun, next to the word re (symbolizing, in a figurative sense, the religious conception of the god Re) is a purely Egyptian term and not of Asiatic origin. It is very ancient, dating as far back as the Middle Kingdom. It is significant that Amon too, in the period of the New Kingdom, tried more and more obviously to absorb all the sun-gods and thus he took on an ever more evident sun character. In opposition to this, the pre-Akhnaton cult of the Aton (still joined with the other sun-gods but sedulously avoiding any identification with Amon) is clearly the creation of the priests of the god Harakhtey, from On (Heliopolis) and the Upper Egyptian On (Hermonthis) if not even, as I consider, some compromise and a concertedly based struggle of the clergy of the sun-worshipping cults against the hegemony of the priesthood of Amon. The priests of Re and Harakhtey considered Amon to be an usurper (mainly, of course, for economic reasons).

As was the long-standing custom in Egypt, towards the end of his reign Amenhotep III summoned his son, Amenhotep IV, to be co-regent in order to ensure the transfer of power to the new government without incident since the surrounding nations were always ready to turn such occasions to their private accounts. Amenhotep III had been sick for a long time and his son governed jointly with him (or rather, for him) for at least nine years if not more (ten to twelve). From childhood, Amenhotep IV had had an opportunity of observing the opinions of his father in regard to the priesthood of Amon and also the opinions of the sun cults' priests who were the enemies of the Amon religion and of their economic hegemony. No matter what were the other personal traits of this young co-regent, his upbringing was directed to inculcating him with his

father's personal despotism. He could not agree with the idea that the king of the most powerful country in the world should divide his power with the High Priest of Amon.

Politically, he sought support from the priesthood of the old sun cults and in this simply continued the trend begun by his father when he held his coronation in Upper Egyptian On and not in the capital, Weseti the city of Amon (and named himself High Priest of the sun-god from On, Re-Harakhtey).

Even if these actions were of a political nature, the first real expression of Amenhotep IV's fight against the priesthood of Amon was conditioned by economic reasons—the king relieved the High Priest of the control of his estates. This was an unheard-of step and one which shows the real reason for later reforms. It was a fight against the economic power of the priesthood of Amon, not only against the Amon religion itself. Hitherto the king's actions in no way contradicted old Egyptian religion; the ideological supremacy of Amenre as King of the Gods had not been infringed upon. The king continued to call himself Amenhotep ("Amon is Satisfied") and to his titles he himself added that of "beloved of Amon." The king's religious convictions developed parallel to his fight in the economic and political fields.

The ruler's main idea was to destroy the political power of the priesthood of Amon by political means and, wherever civic affairs were closely linked with the religious by ideological means as well. Religious ideology is here a means of the economic struggle. Let us look more closely into the different stages of this contest.

At first (as we see from one of his titles as High Priest of Harakhtey), Amenhotep IV continued earlier religious patterns. Aton was for him the name of the god Harakhtey which was formulated as follows: "Harakhtey who rejoices in the land of light in his name, Show (the god of air and light), who is the Aton." Even if we replace, in our translation, the god Show by the word light (or heat) of which Show was the patron god, the identification of the god Harakhtey (portrayed with a human body and a falcon's head, that is, with the head of the falcon-god, Hor) with the sun sphere remains unchanged. Despite this new interpretation of the god, Amenhotep IV still permitted the former portrayals of the Aton as the falcon-headed Harakhtey. Not until the fifth or sixth year of his reign was the Aton portrayed simply as a sun sphere, in other words, as the sun appears and is in reality. Already Amenhotep III had emphasized Truth in his inscriptions, still, however, as the Goddess of Truth, Maat. Amenhotep IV stripped Truth of its ancient mythology and began to make it a reality.

In the new depictions of the Aton we find only one allegory, that of the sun's rays descending from the sun and terminating in hands which sometimes hold the hieroglyphic symbol of the word *"onkh,"* or "life" (the sun as the giver of life). It is here that the real ideological fight against the Amon priesthood really begins.

The latter, of course, did not want to surrender their position and the struggle was therefore accompanied by decisive political measures. The cult of Amon was abolished and its name removed from all public inscriptions throughout the empire. Similarly, the cults of other gods were also abolished, although not with such consistency. The Aton became the only deity and therefore the plural word, "gods," was also removed from inscriptions. As a result of this, there was even an alteration in the king's name. This name, Amenhotep, which meant "Amon is Satisfied," was in contradiction to reality and therefore the king assumed a new name, Akhnaton, which means "He Who is Beneficial to Aton," but not "Aton's Radiance" or even "Aton's Thunder," nor "Spirit of Aton," as has sometimes been claimed.

The new god needed new temples. The king decided to build a new city for his god who was his "father" and of whom he was the sole High Priest and interpreter, and to make it the centre of his empire. He therefore chose a hitherto unsettled site midway on the road between Weset and Mennofer (today at the village of El-Amarie, renamed in error by Egyptologists as Amarna) and in the sixth year of his reign he had the boundaries of the future city marked out by great stelæ. Among the inscriptions carved upon these stones are the names of the constructions to be built in the city of Akhetaton ("Horizon of Aton").

Up till now, Akhnaton had been crowned with success. Amenhotep III, as long as his health still permitted, actively participated in and agreed with the politics of his son and co-regent. Less enthusiastic about the new ideas was the Queen Mother, Tey. We know, for example, that she retained for a long time her old religious convictions, yet without being a friend of Amon. Queen Nefertiti became his close collaborator so that the king's wife assumed a more prominent position in Akhetaton than Tey had ever had in Weset.

With rich gifts, Akhnaton won followers among whom he divided the high state offices. These dignitaries made it all too clear on their tomb inscriptions what had been the main reason for their desertion of Amon—the king's gifts, direct gain and hope of a state career. The king's power was great then and the priests had not yet control of the army, the administrative machinery or of the vice-royalty of Nubia. They were not yet prepared to fight the ruling dynasty as was the case at the end of the new Kingdom when they learned from the example of Akhnaton's "rebellion."

The king's orders were therefore carried out without a murmur and the priesthood's opposition could be crushed. The people, the most important factor in the state, were silent and obeyed. Akhnaton did not even

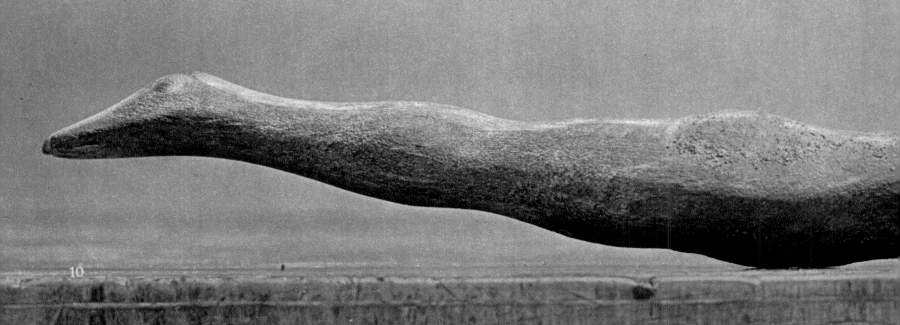

take the people's religion from them. Nor did he take their property, that is, no more than before, but he did take the property of the clergy. For the people, Akhnaton's reforms were only what they were in reality: the fight of the king against economic power veiled by the priesthood of Amon, that is, a fight which did not affect the people in the least and which they did not know how to turn to serve their own interest.

As far as the question of religion is concerned, the people's creed was not with any religious system. This was nurtured by the priests and not by the king. The people believed in legends and superstitions and these the king did not take away from them. Around the king himself, in the village where dwelt the royal craftsmen and artists and those who were building the Akhetaton rock-tombs, the people made amulets and statuettes of protecting gods just as they had always done. (A whole such village was brought by Akhnaton from the royal cemeteries in Weset. After the king's death, they went back to Weset where their descendants in 1169 B. C. organized the first strike recorded in human history.)

It was the same throughout the country. Similarly, the people's religious faith had been limping along for a whole century behind the former official Amon religion. A long time is necessary before a new belief takes root. Akhnaton himself was not so uncompromising. In such a monotheistic religion as that of Aton, there should have been no place for Usire's (Osiris) Empire of the Dead. But despite this, Akhnaton silently permitted the folk legend of the good god Usire, king of the empire of the dead and of immortal life. Thus we find even the king's ushebti figures in which Akhnaton is represented in the classical likeness of the mummified Usire, holding his traditional insignia, a shepherd's crook and a utensil for gathering ladanum (and not a cat o'nine tails or flagellum as was previously often thought).

The only difference between the ushebti figures from the time of the Aton religion and that immediately preceding it, is the name of the king which is now the sole inscription on the statuette, replacing the former magic formulæ. In this and in other cases, the king did not interfere with old customs, trying only to give them another meaning. This of course was such a subtle change that the people were in no way offended.

However, even though Akhnaton was such a clever ruler that he gave the people no reason for discontent, on the other hand he made no attempt to obtain their sympathies or to win them to his side. However much Akhnaton may be congenial to us as a person and however ready we are to recognize that his religious convictions represent a higher and more progressive type of religions we still must not forget that this king fought first of all for his own personal interests.

The big political mistake which Akhnaton committed was his decision to leave the former capital of the empire and move permanently to Akhetaton. The new capital could not be built over night and such

a big city as Weset could not be moved to a new site. But Akhnaton did not want to destroy Weset with its monuments of the past and its mighty constructions put up by his own father. By moving his court, Akhnaton lost his direct influence and surveillance in Weset.

In the eighth year of his reign, Akhnaton made an inspection tour of the construction site and the following year he had already received a visit from his parents in the new royal palace at Akhetaton. Building continued, therefore, at a comparatively rapid rate.

The too-great interest aroused over the construction of the new large city diverted the king's attention from important events which were going on at home and abroad. Akhetaton became for Akhnaton his entire country and it seemed as though now the king, after the apparent consummation of his victory over the Amon clergy, did not want to be bothered by what went on outside the walls of his city dedicated to the Aton.

He was occupied with plans for the building of further monuments, and in the sense mentioned of an attempt to realize a faith in the Truth, he even influenced the court artists of which (according to the report of one of them) he himself became the teacher. And even if the king himself only brought this new trend to a peak it was his personal interest in the putting of his main ideas into practice which was a direct reason for the new and thoroughly realistic direction in art.

This new trend expressed itself in two directions, in form and in choice of subject matter. In regard to the former, the realism was often exaggerated. This is quite natural. It seems as if the artists, not having once satisfied Akhnaton, and afraid of incurring further reproaches, exaggerated reality. In this way some of the royal portraits are clear caricatures.

As far as content of the artistic creations is concerned, reality is stressed by depicting the king in his family circle as he plays with his little daughters or even kissing other members of the family. On the one hand Akhnaton stressed his own divinity even more than his predecessors on the throne (he even had his own High Priest who served him as a god). On the other hand, he forgot (of course still in the interests of Truth) that for his subjects, used to idealizing the king's majesty in statues and reliefs, such portrayals depicting scenes from his family life and with their realistic illustrations of his own natural likeness which were not always very flattering, would make a bad impression. A pleasing element for us in this art is its love for nature

expressed in the unstylized depiction of Egyptian flora and the life-like pictures of animals (although here too, however, we have some much older examples).

All this helped to inspire a reform in the language. The king ordered the use of the contemporary language in literature, replacing classical Egyptian, a living language during the Middle Kingdom and which, until this new decree, had been the official written language and was now an obsolete anachronism.

In the question of dogma, Akhnaton fully developed his convictions separating the Aton from the god Hor in the tenth year of his reign. In his title he retained only the name "Re, ruler of both regions of light" and omitted the name of Hor. "Re" (sun) was explained here as "the father who has re-appeared as the Aton." According to ancient mythology, or rather folk creed, the Sun left the Earth, disgusted with people's behaviour and ascended to the firmament. This definitive conception was expressed by Akhnaton in the form of a hymn by Aton whom he announced as his father. Although the former hymns to the sun, according to the Amenre conception, were, in many a simile and metaphor, startlingly analogous, the main conception is now entirely new, not burdened with mythology but flavoured with genuine awe and thankfulness to the life-giving power of the sun. The king's song to the sun probably makes a far deeper impression on today's reader than it did on the Egyptians of Akhnaton's time. (For lack of space, only the beginning of the song is given here.)

"Beautiful, thou appearest in splendour on the horizon of heaven,
Thou living sun sphere (Aton), origin of life!
When thou art risen on the eastern horizon,
Thou has filled every land with thy beauty;
Thou art lovely, great, glowing high above all lands . . ."

Akhnaton's decision never to leave the limits of Akhetaton had far-reaching consequences. (Akhnaton swore this oath on the boundary stelæ of his new city. He used the word meaning "to cross" which can never be construed to mean "to move" as one Egyptologist has claimed. And even if this were true, the sense of the sentence is that "Akhnaton will never move his headquarters from Akhetaton" and so our contention

remains unchallenged, since Akhnaton really never left Akhetaton until his death.) He was linked with the rest of the world only through his correspondence and through his courtiers whom he had won more through his gifts than as a result of their own convictions or personal leanings. Thus Akhnaton could not know the real condition of his empire. His unfortunate decision kept him from undertaking at least one inspection trip to Asia as Thutmose IV had done; and this at a time when the presence of the king in Asia was more in the interests of the Egyptian supremacy than ever before.

Sharp changes were in the air in regions sparsely settled by Egyptians. Akhnaton did not even send military aid to his Asiatic vassals when, under attack from neighbouring tribes who were also threatening the Egyptian position, they implored him for help. The loss of prestige meant a set-back for the Egyptian rule in Asia even during the reign of Akhnaton and for his immediate successors.

Akhnaton's attitude in regard to international affairs cannot be simply explained by some sort of deep-seated royal pacifism because he behaved in the same apathetic way in regard to dangers which, in earlier times, would have certainly stimulated him to decisive action. The priesthood of Amon, forced from their position, had not been sitting by with their hands in their laps. On the contrary, these priests knew how to use the king's absence from Weset for their own purposes. As far as the king's "pacifism" is concerned, which

14

some scholars have also tried to read into his hymn, it is made very doubtful by a report of an (unsuccessful) military expedition into Asia during Akhnaton's lifetime. The lack of energetic steps in Asia towards the end of Akhnaton's reign spring either from the king's lack of interest in international events or from the internal condition of Egypt which no longer permitted the organization of military expeditions on a large scale.

During the twelfth year of his reign, Akhnaton was visited by the Queen Mother, whose husband, Amenhotep III, had probably by this time been dead about two years. They now settled permanently in Akhetaton and from approximately that time dates the beginning of the end of the Aton religion.

Even if we know that former claims about Akhnaton's supposed illnesses are contradicted by later research or unfounded (like the skeleton of Akhnaton which is, in reality, that of his brother and which in itself shows no traces of illness anyway) and the statues of him do not enable us to judge with any accuracy the state of his health, it is still sufficient to realize that Akhnaton governed only 17 years so that he probably reached the age of 30. Thus he died a young man and still he did not have enough energy to renew his fight against the priesthood of Amon at the most decisive moment.

On the contrary, soon after the twelfth year of his reign, Akhnaton quarrelled with Nefertiti, a loyal defender of the Aton cult, and the queen went into retirement in her palace of Hetaton. Akhnaton summoned his brother, Smenkhkare, to govern with him in the fifteenth year of his reign and sent him with his eldest daughter, the wife of Smenkhkare, to Weset in order to seek a reconciliation with the Amon clergy.

After two years of co-regency, Smenkhkare died, probably soon after the death of Akhnaton. Nefertiti tried shortly after the king's death to save the work of her husband which he himself had been unable to defend, during the last years of his life, due to illness or exhaustion after his earlier struggle for power.

The queen installed Tutankhaton, the youngest brother of Akhnaton, on the throne. But this youthful king soon became a toy in the hands of the Amon priesthood. After three years he changed his name to Tutankhamon and moved to Weset. The Amon priesthood triumphed. Still another attempt was made to confute the plans of the Amon priesthood—following the premature death of Tutankhamon, the king's widow, no other than the youngest daughter of Akhnaton, wrote to the Hittite king, Shupululiuma, asking him to send her his son to be her husband and thus to become king of Egypt. After she had repeated her request, Shupululiuma agreed but the prince was killed en route to Egypt, obviously by order of the High Priest of Amon. The young widow was then forced to take Eye as her husband who thus became king and assumed the religion of Amon, the latter once more becoming the undisputed master of the Egyptian pantheon.

The religious reforms which Akhnaton inaugurated, hardly survived the king's death. The trend of artistic reform can be traced for only a short while and thus only the linguistic reform fully demonstrated its life force.

From all this we can conclude that Akhnaton's driving force in religious reform had been his fight for state power. Perhaps we can best illustrate this contention and at the same time evaluate the significance of the Amarna epoch by briefly taking our stand towards the most typical of the existing opinions.

Even if we do not favour hypothetical considerations we are led to the conjecture that if Akhnaton had really only pursued the ideal goals of religion or if he had wanted "for reasons of statesmanship" to give his empire a universal religion, acceptable to the Asiatic peoples as well (among whom the sun cults are often encountered), he would doubtlessly have achieved his goal far more easily in close co-operation with the priesthood of Amon. Co-operating with them and supporting them, he would have met with no less understanding than he had from the priests of other sun worshippers. After all, the idea that the sun religion, based on the figure of a central god, better served a great empire such as Egypt had become in the 18th dynasty, was the idea of the Amon priests themselves!

The trend towards centralization and unification, towards universalism and syncretism was already seen in the local Weset religion (not sun-worshipping) of Amon which (even before Akhnaton) made Amenre "king of all gods." It is enough only to cite several fragments of a hymn to Amenre which we know for certain was sung before the time of Amarna: "Amenre . . . lord of truth and father of the gods, who created men and beasts, lord of all that is . . . he who made fodder for the cattle and fruit trees for men, he who made that from which the fishes live in rivers and birds in the sky, he who gave breath to that which is inside the egg and gave life to the baby worms, he who made a way of living for the mosquitoes and similarly for serpents and flies, he who made that which the mice need in their holes and the birds in every tree, . . . he who at night keeps watch while all men sleep and cares for the needs of his creations . . . he who made man and made distinctions in their characters, who gave them life, distinguished one from another by their colour, he who hears even the prayer of a prisoner . . . he for love of whom the Nile has come . . ."

What a small step it is from this "one and only, who is without his peer, Amon-Sun," to Akhnaton's Aton, "the only god, besides whom there is none such as he, who made the earth according to his desires, unique!"

The Amenre conception of a central god who was king of all the other gods was, in addition, certainly more acceptable to the non-Egyptian peoples because they had only to identify their sun gods with Amenre (as later the Greeks themselves identified Re with their Helios); they would have been permitted to continue to worship other gods of local origin over whom Amenre would have become king but would not have abolished them.

The reason for Akhnaton's reforms was not the above-mentioned idea of unity which he did not invent anyway but accepted from other sources. Because he did not link his efforts with those of the Amenre priests, his motives for reform must have been different. The way his religious convictions developed and formed during his reign parallel to his fight against the priesthood of Amon, in which he had from the outset to move into the economic and political fields, clearly corresponds to our explanation.

We do not believe, on the other hand, that the religious reforms were mere camouflage for Akhnaton and that he did not believe in the ideas which he himself promulgated. There is no doubt about his credo. The king's object from the outset was absolute state power: his religious faith was in reality a constantly developing instrument to achieve his aims but not that sort of instrument which is used and then discarded after it has served its purpose. The king's religion grew out of the faith of his father which was common for this time, being influenced by the priests of On. But this religion developed, gradually becoming a more perfect product of the fight against the priesthood of Amon and of his determination to be the sole master of Egypt as his ancestors were before the priesthood had grown into an over-important factor in the state.

But Akhnaton was not a man who achieved his aims only through outward acts. He was a thinker who motivated his acts, joining the impulses of the outside world with their reflexes in his internal world of thought. He doubtless joined the means with the ends in an inseparable entity. But if at the beginning he was a man of action, the thinker-theoretician assumed ascendancy. The outward reasons for his failures have been presented above. His real greatness as a personality, how-ever, consists of the fact that he was one of the first philosophers on the throne, one of the first kings of ancient times whose intellectual life superseded the crudely materialist interests of the kings of his period.

The fact that the basis on which Akhnaton built was not exclusively his intellectual creation, naturally does not diminish his greatness. We admire his accurate observa-tions of nature (a wonderful proof is an excerpt from the Akhnaton hymn where the king correctly observes that a little bird cheeps in the egg even before it is hatched; modern naturalists fully agree with this observation) and we admire his tendency to separate mythological superstitions and obscurantism from reality and to create a truthful picture of natural phenomena and truthfully depict nature in the arts.

Akhnaton's ability to apply his convictions of truth and reality in the different branches of human activity was especially admirable, as was his ability to put his convictions into practice despite obdurate traditionalism and his reactionary environ-ment. Akhnaton realized the danger arising from the opportunistic priesthoods who used for their own interests obscure lies of magic and untruthful oracular utterances by the Amon statue, as we learn of these practices from sources of those times when later the priesthood of Amon regained firm power. The king did not realize that if his theories were to triumph, they must first help to bring some good to the people. We cannot, however, blame Akhnaton too much for this fault; the king's life was too short and the time was not yet ripe. But even so, Akhnaton was an enthusiastic fighter for truth and an admirable figure among the kings who sat on the Egyptian throne.

This short study of the Amarna epoch was initiated after the discovery of the ushebti figure (a statuette which represents the deceased and which was supposed to come to life in the under-world and do work for the dead person) which is reproduced in the photographs in this book.

The statuette is of dark blue faience, 13.2 centimetres high. The face of the statuette immediately suggests a resemblance to Akhnaton but the hieroglyphic inscription reads: "He to whom eternal life is given, Oakheperre, deceased, son of Re . . ." The first king's name in the cartouche, Oakheperre, is not the prenomen of Akhnaton whose name was Neferkheprure. The second name is, unfortunately,

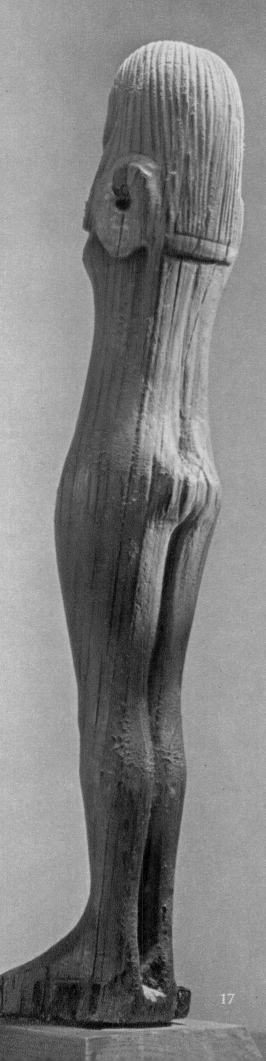

17

illegible, and only the sun symbol is visible which can represent either the word "Re" or the determinative of the word "Aton." The statuette is especially interesting because of this inscription. Up to a certain date only two inscriptions were known which referred to the son of Amenhotep III, Oakheperre. Later it was discovered that the name in the first inscription should read Ankhkheprure, which is the prenomen of Smenkhkare. From this it was judged that also Mr. Davies' reading of the second inscription is incorrect and that here too was a sign representing the word "onkh" and not "oa" which would mean that no Oakheperre ever existed and that in both cases the prenomen in question was that of Smenkhkare.

Assuming that the statuette is authentic, there are two main alternatives. The family resemblance is clear, thus it could only be one of Akhnaton's brothers. Of these, Tutankhamon is excluded, so it is either the almost unknown brother, Oakheperre, who, judging from his face, had reached adulthood and become king, even though for a short while. Or else Smenkhkare was using the form Oakheperre instead of his prenomen Ankhkheprure, and in this case the statuette represents Smenkhkare. Thus the second cartouche inscription would in that case be Nefernefruaton or Smenkhkare (both are acknowledged forms of the second name [*nomen*] of Akhnaton's brother).

The existence of Oakheperre, a king unknown until now, from the Amarna epoch, would come as a great surprise. But such a possibility cannot be ruled out because there is very little information even about Smenkhkare himself.

I have given the conclusions which could be reached "assuming that the statuette is authentic." In disagreement with such an assumption, there seems to be the fact of the unusual order of the initial words of the inscription which is usually read after the name of the king himself, i. e. as an adjective (e.g. A, Son of Re, B, To Whom Life is Given). Even though the reverse order in the inscription is unusual, from the point of view of language it is not impossible since the relative clause on a participial base can have the validity of a substantive in Egyptian ("He, to Whom Life is Given"). For the time being the question of the authenticity of this ushebti figure must be left open.

Zbyněk Žába

18

2. Ushebti figure with the features of King Akhnaton and with the prenomen Oacheperré. Detail, blue glazed earthernware with brownish-violet spots; inscription on front side, New Kingdom, about 1350 B. C., height of whole Ushebti 13.2 cm., height of head 2.5 cm., private collection (see Nos 4, 5, 23, 24).

4. Ushebti figure as No 2, right profile (see Nos 2, 5, 23, 24).

5. Ushebti figure as No 2, left profile (see Nos 2, 4, 23, 24).

6. Torso. Black stone, Late Period (about 600 B. C.), height 6 cm., private collection (see No 7).

7. Torso, as No 6.

8. Miniature sarcophagus (with woooden mummy inside). Polychrome wood. Middle Kingdom(?), 9 × 9 × 25 cm. National Gallery, Prague.

10. Spoon for cosmetics. Form of swimming girl, wood with remnants of polychromy, New Kingdom (about 1350 B. C.), length 34 cm., private collection (see No 51).

12. Boat for the Dead. Wood with remnants of polychromy. Middle Kingdom, length 68 cm., Náprstek Museum, Prague.

14. Jackal with ostrich feather. Wood with remnants of polychromy, New Kingdom (about 1200 B. C.), length 27.6 cm., private collection.

16. Statuette of young girl. Wood. New Kingdom (about 1300 B. C.), height 28 cm., private collection (see Nos 17, 38).

17. Statuette of a girl, as No 16.

18. Statuette of a girl. Bronze, green patina. New Kingdom (about 1250 B. C.), height 24.5 cm., private collection (see No 50).

21. Sacred bird Ibis. Bronze, Late Period (about 600 B. C.), height 9 cm., private collection.

23. Ushebti figure as No 1, whole *en face*. Fragment of stele in background (see Nos 2, 4, 5, 24).

24. Ushebti figure as No 1, head *en face*, height of face 1.6 cm. (see Nos 2, 4, 5, 23).

25. Head of a king. The lid of a sarcophagus, granite. Middle Kingdom(?), height 55 cm., National Museum, Prague.

26. Egyptian cobra (Naja haje). Depicting the protective goddess of Egyptian kings, Wedjoyet (probably from headband), bronze with brown patina (New Kingdom[?]), height 10 cm., private collection.

27. Lid of funeral vessel with head of king. Limestone with remnants of polychromy. Possibly Old Kingdom, height 11.7 cm., private collection.

28. Lid of funeral vessel with head of king, as No 27.

29. Lid of funeral vessel with head of king, as No 27.

30. Cat. The sacred animal of the Goddess Bastet, bronze with beautiful green patina. Late period (about 600 B. C.), height with stand 10.5 cm., height of cat itself 8.5 cm., private collection.

31. Oarsman in boat. Polychrome wood. Middle Kingdom (the beginning of the 2nd millenium B. C.), length of boat 35 cm., Náprstek Museum, Prague (see No 32).

32. Oarsman in boat as No 31.

34. Egyptian sacrificing a ram. Detail, limestone, remnants of polychromy, New Kingdom (about 13th century B. C.), height 16 cm., private collection (see No 35).

35. Sacrificant as No 34, whole profile.

36. Egyptian king offering sacrifice. Detail, wood with remnants of white paint, Late Period (about 600 B. C.), total height 46 cm., private collection (see Nos 37, 38).

37. King offering sacrifice, as No 36, whole.

38. King offering sacrifice, as No 36, head, profile.

39. Statuette of girl, as No 16, detail.

40. Statuette of girl. (In background part of relief tomb decoration). Head and limbs from ivory, trunk from ebony. Late Period (about 600 B. C.), probable height of whole figure 18 cm., height of preserved, i.e. re-produced part 15 cm., private collection.

42. Statuette of girl, as No 40, detail.

43. Head of Isis. Relief of diorite, Middle Kingdom(?), height 32 cm., National Museum, Prague.

44. Statuette of girl. Detail, polychrome limestone, New Kingdom (about 13th century B. C.), height 38.5 cm., private collection (see Nos 45, 47).

45. Statuette of girl, as No 44, detail of head.

46. Double coffin with mummy of a young girl from noble family, New Kingdom (about 1300 B. C.), Moravská Třebová Museum.

47. Statuette of girl, as in No 45, whole.

48. Towret, goddess of fertility. Pendant, blue glazed clay. Middle Kingdom, height 6 cm., private collection.

49. Head of an Egyptian king. Limestone, remnants of poly-chromy, Middle Kingdom, 12th dynasty (about 1800 B. C.), height 11.5 cm., private collection.

50. Statuette of girl, as No 18, detail.

51. Spoon for cosmetics, as in No 10. Detail of head, remnants of painting on eyes, cheeks and mouth. Photo-graphed in the ultra-violet spectrum (see No 10).

52. Isis offering a sacrifice. Fragment from mummy case, New Kingdom (about 13th century B. C.), height 22 cm., private collection.

24

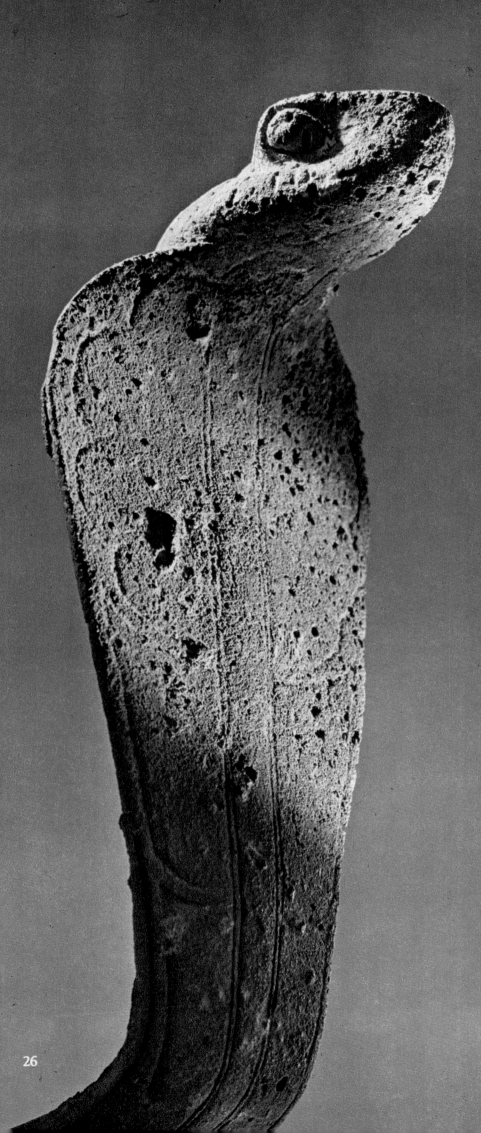

34

36

44

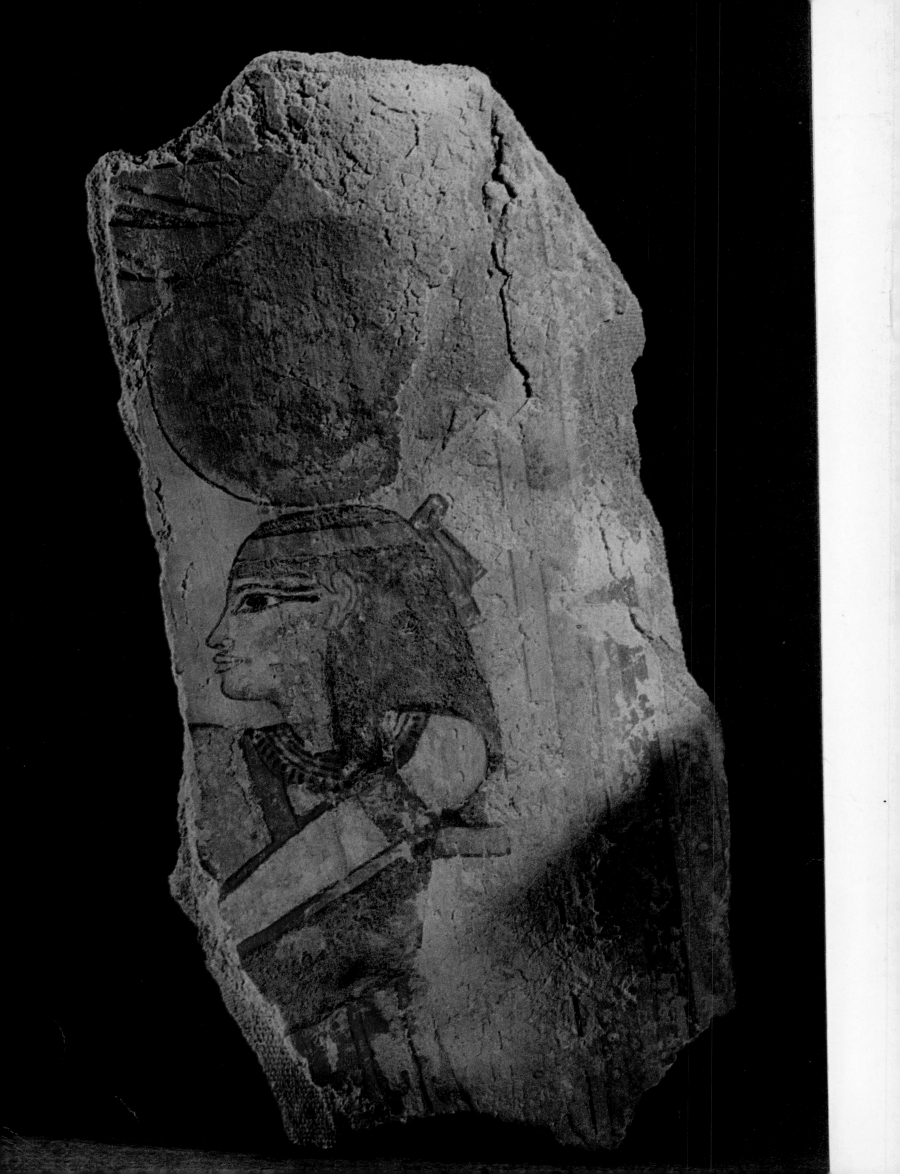

WHEN AT DAWN YOU HAVE COME OUT AGAIN UNTO THE HORIZON
AND ALL DAY YOU SHINE AS A BALL OF FIRE
WHEN YOU HAVE ROUTED DARKNESS AND GIVE US YOUR RAYS
BOTH LANDS ARE AS IF IT WERE A FEAST
PEOPLE HAVE WAKENED AND ARE UP ON THEIR FEET
BECAUSE YOU HAVE ROUSED THEM
THEY WASH AND THEY DRESS
AND LIFT UP THEIR ARMS IN GREETING TO YOUR FIERY COMING

THE WHOLE LAND GOES ABOUT ITS WORK.
THE CATTLE ARE ALL PLEASED WITH THEIR PASTURES
THE TREES AND PLANTS ARE GREENING
AND THE WINGS OF THE BIRDS LEAVING THEIR NESTS
ARE SPREAD OUT IN A GREETING TO YOU.
THE SMALLER BEASTS ARE ALL JUMPING ON THEIR LEGS
AND WHATEVER FLIES AND RISES IN FLIGHT
ARE ALIVE BECAUSE OF YOUR COMING.
SHIPS ARE SAILING UP STREAM AND DOWN
FOR ALL ROADS ARE OPEN BECAUSE OF YOUR FIERY COMING
AND THE FISH IN THE RIVER ARE JUMPING AT YOUR FACE

FOR YOUR RAYS PENETRATE EVEN THE DEPTHS OF THE GREAT GREEN
SEA.

From the Achnaton solar myth.

Africa

The Masks

THE MASKS AND WOOD-CARVINGS
OF THE AFRICAN NEGROES

The art of the African Negroes began to interest Europeans about a century ago, in the first place of course as ethnographical material. Frobenius' work from the latter part of the last century has afforded us most information on this subject. During the present century the artistic quality of the work of the Negroes has begun to make itself felt. Artists and a few collectors were the first willingly to consider African collections purely as an artistic expression but in spite of all efforts theoretical work has slipped into ethnographical diagrams and psychological-religious explanations, and into considerations as to its metaphysical importance (e.g. E. v. Sydow). Not even some of the more recent works have been able to get away from idealistic fantasies to a more objective explanation (L. Underwood). Only in rare cases have progressive attempts been made at explaining African art on the basis of economic factors (H. Kühn) or from an inborn race instinct formed by the historical development of individual tribes (Gaffé). Works attempting a systematic classification of material and knowledge of African art from the artistic-scientific point of view have been few and far between (Einstein, Sweng, Kyersmeir, etc.).

Present-day knowledge is still too limited to allow of a chronological classification and explanation of the development of African art. There is no doubt that this art has a very old tradition even though attempts at tracing some of its forms from ancient Egyptian art will probably remain speculative. Literary documents mention sculpture done by African Negroes in the 14th and 15th centuries (Ibn Batuta and A. Malfonte). The Englishman B. Fagg recently excavated in northern Nigeria terra-cotta statues which, according to geological data, could date back to the period before Christ. The famous Yorubian statues from Ife, discovered by Frobenius are now thought to date to the 12th century (Frobenius was of the opinion that they are older while Einstein placed them in the 15th century); at this time the famous tradition of Benin bronzes probably began. The portraits of Bushong (Bakub) chiefs go back to 1600. Of course, the overwhelming majority of Negro art works must be considered as recent, if not contemporary work.

In classifying African art according to regions or tribes we get onto surer ground even though we are often dependent on guesswork and come up against lack of agreement in the opinions of experts. There is no doubt that as regards quantity and artistic quality first place is held by the region of West Africa, i.e. the coastal zone from Senegambia in the north, across Guinea, Sierra Leone, Liberia, the Ivory Coast, the Gold Coast, Togo, Dahomey, Nigeria, the Cameroons, Gabun and the Congo to Angola in the south. In general, it may be said that West-African art reaches its peak in Nigeria (Yoruba and Benin), in the Cameroons and in central and south-western Belgian Congo (BaKuba, BaLuba, Urua, etc.). As regards subject matter this art includes everything from figures and masks to utilitarian wood-carving, stone sculpture, bronzes, wood and terra-cotta. The East-African region, from which in addition to utilitarian art we know figural wood-carvings (for the most part unplastic and lifeless), is far less important, both as regards quality and quantity. But even here we find successful attempts at realistic portrayal. From South Africa the most important works of art are utilitarian carvings with naturalistic animal motifs and primitive bush engravings. In the north, Negro art has greatly succumbed to Arab influence.

It is quite understandable that to collectors masks have always been the most popular feature of all the art of the African Negroes. They are fantastically rich in expression and their total conception and stylization give them a decorative character even if they were not originally intended merely for purposes of ornamentation. These masks are to this day made by wood-carvers who are nearly always peasants and who turn their artistic skill to this work in their free time or to make some extra money, as they themselves admit. The profession is handed down from father to son or other near relative. The master wood-carver takes on apprentices for two or three years. The agreed wages are only paid after the apprenticeship is up and the apprentice must work for his master in the house or in the field during this time. All that is produced by the apprentice during this period belongs to the master.

Women do not participate in wood-carving. The men claim that they are incapable of mastering this art and that it is sufficient for them to know how to make pottery and murals on the clay walls of their huts.

The Negro artists use only hard wood for making the masks. Soft wood quickly rots in tropical climates. The finished carvings take on their black patina by being submerged for a time in the river mud or by being rubbed with leaves from a certain type of vine or with a powder made of charcoal and cinders. The polish is achieved by oiling the blackened wood.

The masks are dyed a dark blue by the cooked leaves of a certain bush and the red colour is obtained by rubbing with berry juice. Otherwise the masks are dyed with red earth, chalk or seared with a hot iron. Where European civilization has not yet penetrated masks are made with three utterly primitive iron instruments.

The Negroes have many legends about the origin of these masks. On the Ivory Coast, for instance, the following tale is told: Once upon a time a hunter fell asleep on the banks of a river. When he awoke he saw a number of water animals had emerged from the river and were dancing on the shore, wearing beautiful masks. The hunter shot at the animals which hastily cast off their masks and disappeared again into the water. He took the masks back to his village and taught his tribesmen the dances which he had watched the animals perform.

All African masks are used for dances. The medicine men too, when they are summoned to cure someone who is sick, wear masks as they dance around the patient's bedside. Each mask represents some special spirit or demon, good or bad, and the wearer of the mask is transformed into this spirit when he dons the mask, as is the case in curing sickness, at funerals, at the celebrations of circumcision and coming-of-age, prophecy-making and the like. The men who wear the masks are always the best dancers.

Some masks are made small, for covering only the face, while others are large enough to conceal the entire head. Others again are small enough for the dancer to hold in his hand. All of them, whether made of wood, skins, reeds or tree-bark, or even sometimes of metal or ivory, have an expression of total repose. That is why the removal of their ornamental feathers, bark fibres and grass, which is linked with the dancer's costume, makes the masks seem, for some observers seeing them in a museum case, static and lifeless. They lack the movement and rhythm of the dance.

But in the dance, worn by costumed native dancers, in the heat of the tropical sun, in the clear moonlight or by the shimmering sparks of a camp-fire, the masks come to life in a strange way. Their "mobile stiffness" fascinates not only the native peoples but European observers as well. The African people believe that the dancer is not their tribesman but a spirit, a demon or a dead ancestor whom the mask represents and who has returned among them in the clamour of celebration, among spectators dizzied by the beats of the tom-tom and the monotonous chanting.

Joe Hloucha

56. Mask from Belgian Congo— The Bapenda Tribe. From ceremonial usage in circumcision, polychrome wood with inserted fragments of mirror on the forehead and cheeks, hornlike protuberances on the head, beard made of tree bark, helmet type of mask covering the entire head down to the shoulders, height 50 cm., depth 35 cm., private collection.

61. Mask from the Ivory Coast—The Dan Tribe. Wood, plaited human hair, teeth of inlaid metal, height 25.7 cm., private collection.

62. Mask from Liberia—The Dan Tribe. Possibly in the image of a gorilla, wood crudely worked over, height 31.5 cm., private collection.

63. Mask from Liberia—The Dan Tribe. Possibly in the image of a gorilla, wood with bits of feather decoration, movable lower jaw, height 31 cm., private collection.

64. Mask from Ivory Coast—The Dan Tribe. Wood with an oily polish through usage, height 26.5 cm., private collection (see No 65).

65. Mask from Ivory Coast—The Dan Tribe, as No 64, detail.

66. Mask from Belgian Congo — The Bayaka Tribe. Probably the spirit of the forest, polychrome wood and bark, height 39 cm., Náprstek Museum, Prague.

67. Mask from Belgian Congo — The Bayaka Tribe. Portrayal of the spirit of the forest, polychrome wood with bast, height 34.7 cm., Náprstek Museum, Prague.

68. Mask from Belgian Congo—The Bayaka Tribe (detail). Figure of a woman made from leather, wood and hair, height 43 cm, Náprstek Museum, Prague (see No 69).

69. Mask, as No 68. Whole.

70. Mask from the Cameroons. Buffalo, wood, height 53.5 cm., Náprstek Museum, Prague.

71. Mask from the Cameroons. Antelope, polychrome wood, height 27 cm., private collection.

72. Mask from Nigeria—The Yoruba Tribe (detail). Polychrome wood, scratches to indicate tatooing, height of the entire mask 37 cm., Náprstek Museum, Prague.

73. Mask from Ivory Coast—The Dan Tribe. Possibly a lion, wood with remnants of white paint, mane of monkey skin, height 33 cm., Náprstek Museum, Prague.

74. Mask from Soudan. Black wood. Height 57 cm., private collection.

75. Mask from West Africa — The Bashileli Tribe. Polychrome wood. Height 43 cm., private collection.

76. Mask possibly from Ivory Coast. Antelope, coloured wood, height 43 cm., private collection.

74

WHEN GOD IN THE DIM PAST CREATED
HE CREATED THE SUN
AND IT RISES, GOES DOWN AND RISES AGAIN
HE CREATED THE MOON
AND IT RISES, GOES DOWN AND RISES AGAIN
HE CREATED MAN
AND HE RISES, GOES DOWN – NEVER TO RISE AGAIN

East Africa, Dink. Tribe.

Africa
The Applied Art

THE APPLIED ART OF AFRICA

If at some time a complete world history of applied art should be published, the contributions of the primitive countries would be exhausted in a few short paragraphs. And these at best would be limited to hypotheses and more or less artificial constructions. However, should such an encyclopedia be predominantly a picture catalogue, the overwhelming majority of the material would deal precisely with primitive art. Moreover, the applied art of the primitive African nations would unquestionably be in the forefront—not only in number but principally in the inexhaustible wealth of ingenuity shown by their works.

The statement seems paradoxical—but justified, nonetheless. In other words, we are confronted with an enormous complex of art works whose historical evolution up to the present is in veiled ignorance but whose inventive and emotional appeal in many aspects far surpasses the art of higher civilized countries. Primitive art and particularly that of Africa, although possibly based on ancient cultural heritages, is freer, more direct in its expression and lighter, so light that it sometimes borders on a sort of recklessness. The bold certainty of the African artist, his instinctive ability to grasp the essential in a brief statement, and an infinite source of inspiration which is his through an intimate contact with a free and unrestrained nature—all this forms the basis for a wide application of art in the production of useful objects. We find here the whole gamut of contradictions: from creations which are at times naively formalistic to works whose content is so profound emotionally that they compel us again and again to the question whether a mythical humus of ancient cultural heritages did not provide the soil for this strangely beautiful flora. In this art we find an abundance of everything, and yet one thing would be vainly sought for: surfeit or boredom. It is an art fresh, vital and capricious like a child—animated and animating, but thoroughly unsophisticated.

It may be objected that it is incorrect to speak of applied art where practically speaking non-functional fine art is unknown. If we do so, it is in order to distinguish the art of various cults (masks for cult dances, fetishes for witchcraft and religious ceremonials, independent figures for ancestor worship and so forth) from that art which has nothing or very little in common with this type of creative expression bound as it is to tradition and ritual, that is, from that art which arises spontaneously out of the creation of profane objects for daily use. Applied art in this case is not merely an addition tagged on to the objects of physical utility but is in itself the daily requirement of the primitive man. The æsthetic quality is in perfect harmony with the object itself, indeed, without it the latter is unthinkable, forming always a unified whole. Perhaps it is this very fact that the primitive artist creates his works with a clear notion of their utilitarian values which gives them a greater effectiveness from an artistic point of view. Only thus is it possible to explain the fact that in the simplest works (spoon p. 89, comb p. 80) we find high artistic virtues; and on the other hand, in the works more ingenious, decorative and at times more impressive artistically, there are always marks of utility, even though reduced to a certain functionalism (bronze Benin panel, etc.).

The spoon or soup-ladle brilliantly carved in ivory is a typical illustration of African applied art (pl. 89). It is a beautifully furled leaf (or fruit?) which is being chased after by a rodent called *sangu* in the native dialect. The formal aspect and the functionalism are components of a single æsthetic effect. At first glance it is evident . that the animal though considerably stylized is truly a living creature, that mother nature herself inspired the native artist. Quite intentionally he placed the main emphasis in the typical characteristics of the animal by means of a proportional enlargement of the claws achieving thereby not only a wonderful and highly dramatic appearance of the animal itself but also an increase in the handle surface. With deep, fully plastic carving the artist worked toward gaining a maximum of expressiveness without destroying the characteristic unity of the whole.

Our medicine basket (Plate No 90) illustrates the high level of taste achieved by the primitive artist. No European artist would be ashamed of its beautifully simple decoration, the sharp angles and horizontal lines of which correspond to the base and the crown of the lid, or its general outline.

An odd idea so completely devoid of all conventions: such is our "walking vessel" (Plate No 91). The carving in wood, which takes on an exquisite resemblance to a basket of woven reeds as a result of the treatment of the surface, is a perfect personification of the fairy tale theme of the pot of sustenance (the pot going out into the world), familiar perhaps to every country of the world in countless variations. It is neither certain nor important whether this work in fact deals with that particular fairy-tale pot. Germane to our discussion, however, is the fact that the artist succeeded in alluding to the sense of the theme so that the vessel is really walking. And this effect was realized with the simplest means, so simple that we would be obliged to look for a long time in the art of civilized countries before we find a similar form; every artist would certainly indicate at least the upper limbs, if not the face. It is nor a vessel remodelled into some sort of animal, neither is it a disfigured man but simply a vessel unto itself, hobbling along rather stiffly in accordance with its cylinder-like body.

Our next vessel, or rather little jug (Plate No 92), is conceived quite differently. It belongs to the rare group of unfired clay vessels of the Yeruba tribe (Benin?) and therefore to the inheritors of an ancient cultural heritage which archeological studies have demonstrated in the exquisite terra-cotta heads from Ife. The vessel is interesting from a technical point of view. The bottom is formed by a tough, fibre-like plate which is covered on both sides, that is, inside and outside, by a layer of clay. On this then the body is literally built up from six vertical parts pressed into form. The resulting fissures were retouched and finally the vessel was reinforced once more on the inside by a thick layer of clay. Vapourizing substances (oils?) that provided further strength were added to the clay whereby considerable hardness and resistance against moisture were obtained. From the fact that in order to elaborate a repeated plastic decoration the component parts were pressed into a negative form (perhaps also clay), it may be assumed that ours is not a single independent piece but simply one of a series of identical or similar vessels. Without doubt it originally had a folding lid.

A native chieftain (seen from the front) standing on an elephant(?), in fact an elephant's head, forms the dominant figure and the only break in an otherwise endless belt of relief decorations. Its hands raised, it reminds one of a caryatid supporting the catch of a pot cover. Plant leaves are found on both sides of the elephant's head, evidently indicating vegetation. Into this scheme a series of human figures, possibly warriors, which encompass the entire body of the vessel, are worked in. Above them is a horizontal belt decorated with the emblem of man's common bond of solidarity; in this case it may symbolize that element which holds so much mystery for the natives: the bewilderment of the jungles. Over the symbol and probably in contemplated relation to it hover indecipherable forms representing either mystic birds or, more probably, spirits that live on the tops of sacred trees.

From an artistic point of view the main interest is centered in the spatial arrangement of the decorations as a whole. They are

composed almost exclusively of horizontal and vertical axes. The latter especially together with the general outline of the vessel enables us to determine the ancient prototype of all primitive vessels (at least insofar as the people live in regions covered with rich vegetation): namely, a hollow fruit, most frequently of the gourd-bearing family, the horizontal ridges of which often provided such advanced peoples as the Chinese, Indians, Mexicans and others, with a basic design. Small insect wings are embedded in the clay of the vessel which suggests that it was not fired.

The third vessel, a bowl for betel, is a representative example of the extensive contribution of West African art. We find here an interesting composition which a European artist would be rarely capable of solving, namely, two apparently discordant elements: a figure sculpture and an independent, usually quite simple, vessel. It cannot be denied that each of the two elements when considered independently has its own reason, purpose and sense. And yet when both are brought together, they present a complete whole, a whole not merely richer numerically by the addition of one to the other but richer in content and more expressive. In the case of our illustration, the theme is a chieftain riding home with his booty, or carrying a gift or sacrifice on his head. Elsewhere, the native artist carved a kneeling woman with a child on her back. When viewed in relation to the bowl, we see her then just as she is raising or lowering the heavy load. In short, the piece of sculpture in association with the utilitarian function gains something, expresses more and unwittingly broadens the theme. It is a unique trait of the African artists that they are able to link together elements, which are at times quite disparate, without hesitation and with a certain capriciousness.

The tribal thrones (Plate No 95, 97, 99) as well as the stand for a game with shell, fish *kauri*-called *Mangala* (Plate No 98) which is passionately played throughout the entire African continent, are part of a large group of art works which although not directly serving the ancestor cult are, nevertheless, connected with it. The human figures depicted here represent either outstanding personalities (as is evident from the chieftains' attributes—absence of hair and a single sharpened tooth), or simply the figures of ancestors, usually of both sexes. Two pairs of figures are seated on our thrones which illustrate beautifully the succession of generations. Especially on the thrones (Plate No 99) the idea of the present generations being borne by those of the past is superbly rendered by the neat construction of the seat.

The following round throne (Plate No 97) is conceived differently and, therefore, when seen from the front cannot offer the same view; the profile, however, is more impressive. Just as in the previous work, it relates a message which is quite intelligible: the past generations bear the present. This concept is the source of inspiration for the uncomplicated thinking of the primitive artist.

Conceivably this throne as a type may be older than the two previous ones not only because of the more primitive iconography of the figures but principally because it reveals the original prototype: a cylindrical piece of trunk from which by a gradual deepening of the initial shallow carving the present pierced work evolved, exceedingly complex in technique. Only then could it in its further development adhere to the type which was so clearly formulated and which so thoroughly disregarded the original roundness of the material as the first throne. Both of the thrones, like the majority of them, are carved from a single piece of wood and despite relatively narrow structures (legs, etc.) are extraordinarily firm and stable.

The little art-ware seemingly so prosaic as our comb (Plate No 80) ideally unites two aims: a decoration and an object of daily use. It is a comb and simultaneously a figure sculpture. And we would not be far from the truth if we say that it more or less portrays its owner, or more precisely, that it depicts the ideal type of woman in the Angola tribe to whose intriguing art production this comb belongs. The typical hairdress of the tribal beauties, which is considerably worn with use but still presenting

a handsome face with its olive-like outline, the wittily utilized foreign material (metal rings around the neck), and the handle fashioned into a sort of body, the ornamentation which suggests the local pattern of dress—all this is instilled into a masterful piece of utilitarian art with a playful elegance.

The variety of creative ideas can well be seen from the huge numbers of kitchen utensils. These include bowls, pots, cups and, in particular, spoons and ladles. Apart from the already mentioned spoon with the Sangu animal, we have selected two others (pp. 102, 103) that show the vitality with which their creator has tackled the simple problem of making a spoon out of a piece of wood.

This can be demonstrated especially on the spoon on page 102. The break in its handle is not accidental—together with the heavier end, it is intended to balance the weight of the filled lower part. Its elegant shape contrasts with the more toy-like conception of the ladle with snakes. While that is a naive creation, copied from Nature, the one with the human face is far more complex in its abstract-looking outline. It is probably one of the spoons used in one of the many African rites, wherefore the face on its handle is not a mere ornament, but is symbolically linked with the rite itself.

Space does not permit us to describe the wide variety of working techniques, the materials used (from wood, horn, shells, tree barks, stone and metal up to ivory), and above all the immense number of creative ideas. For that reason we have selected only these few examples to represent this interesting sphere of African applied art.

The antelope (p. 104) may be a toy, or it may also be a hunter's fetish. The rectangular axes of the back and horns lend the animal a kind of immobility—it stands and stares.

This small piece of wood depicts, even though by childish means, seconds in the life of a big animal. Only a hunter who was at the same time also an artist could portray those few brief moments of hesitation before the startled animal seeks safety in wild flight.

In conclusion I wish to mention the Ashanti gold dust weights which for their variety and naive charm are typical products of the primitive African artists. Their yearning to beautify everything with which they come into daily contact is so vital that all of their works, even something so modest as the weights, bear traces of this art, smelling of the damp land and heated by the hot sun.

Bedřich Forman

80. Comb from Angola. Wood with wire, height 15.3 cm., private collection.

82. Weight in the form of a monkey from Gold Coast—the Ashanti Tribe. Used by natives for weighing gold dust; brass-like metal, height 3.8 cm., private collection.

83. Weight in the form of a bird from Gold Coast—the Ashanti Tribe. Used by natives for weighing gold dust, brass-like metal, height 4.8 cm., private collection.

84. Weights in the form of a jaguar and crocodile from Gold Coast—the Ashanti Tribe. Brass-like metal, length 6.2 and 5.5 cm., private collection.

86. Weight in the form of a fish from Gold Coast—the Ashanti Tribe. Used by the natives for weighing gold dust, brass-like metal, length 3.5 cm., private collection.

89. Spoon in the form of the mythical animal Sangu from Ubangi—the Yakoma Tribe. Ivory with reddish-brown patina, length 11 cm., private collection.

90. Case from Portuguese East Africa. Natural and brown-coloured bast, height 20 cm., diam. 9.5 cm., private collection.

91. Vessel on legs from Belgian Congo—the Bakuba Tribe. Black-stained wood, height 21 cm., private collection.

92. Pitcher from Nigeria—the Yoruba Tribe. Dried clay, dark-brown colour, in places dark-red. Height 16 cm., diam. 10 cm., private collection (see No 93).

93. Pitcher as in No 92, side with figures of warriors.

94. Bowl for betel from Nigeria—the Yoruba Tribe. Polychrome wood, height 27 cm., diam. 21 cm., Náprstek Museum, Prague.

95. Chieftain's chair from Angola(?). Wood dyed in place, height 95 cm., Náprstek Museum, Prague.

96. Chieftain's chair from Western Africa. Wood, height 52 cm., diam. 36 cm., private collection.

97. Chieftain's chair from Cameroons. Height 43 cm., diam. 35-39 cm., private collection.

98. Game of mangala—from Belgian Congo. Reddish-brown wood, height 51 cm., private collection (see No 100).

99. Chieftain's chair from Belgian Congo. Hard wood, height 90 cm., maximum width 50 cm., private collection (see No 101).

100. Game of mangala as in No 98, detail of male figure.

101. Chair as in No 99, detail of figure of man with pipe.

102. Wooden spoon. Cameroons, height 27 cm., Náprstek Museum, Prague.

103. Wooden spoon. Golden Coast—The Ashanti Tribe. Length 44 cm., Náprstek Museum, Prague.

104. Figure of an antelope(toy?) from South-East Africa. Wood, height 17,5 cm., private collection.

91

94

98

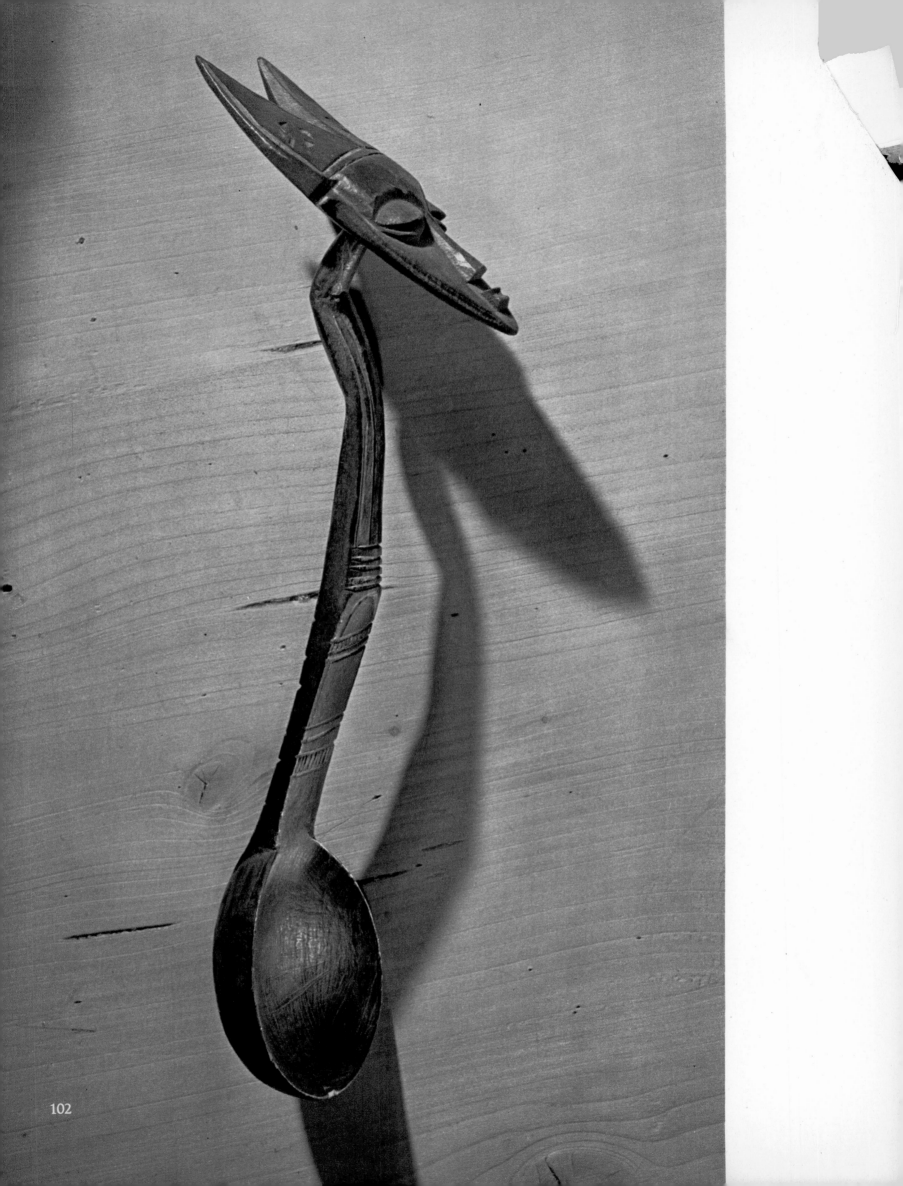

MY EYES ARE RIMMED WITH BLACK ANTIMONY
I HAVE GIRDLED MYSELF WITH AMULETS
I WANT TO QUENCH MY THIRST FOR LOVE
OH YOU, MY SLENDER BOY!

I GO BEHIND THE WALL
I PUT A CLOTH ON MY BREASTS
I SHALL KNEAD BEAUTIFUL CLAY
I SHALL WHITEN THE HOUSE OF MY FRIEND
OH YOU, MY SLENDER BOY!

I SHALL TAKE A SILVER COIN
I SHALL BUY A PIECE OF CLOTH
I SHALL PUT ON MY AMULETS
I SHALL QUENCH MY THIRST FOR LOVE
A HORN OF ANTIMONY IN MY HAND
OH YOU, MY SLENDER BOY!

A song of the Bagirmirs of Soudan.

Africa

The Sculptures

AFRICAN ART COLLECTIONS AND CZECH EXPLORERS

With the passage of time the masks, fetishes and fantastic figures of African carvings have become a familiar sight even in wintry zones. They have become collectors' items, decorations for Central European homes and the subject of special art study. And although Africa itself became known to the same extent as the contribution of its sculptures and although it enters almost daily into the mainstream of our life, we lose sight of its immediate connection with the art relics. It is as though it entered through another door, a door opened to us by the radio, newspapers and ordinary conversations on current events.

At a time when the African continent and African art were the most remote and when Africa had not yet crystallized in our minds as an articulated complex—political, economic and cultural—both were viewed in their intimate relationship. Then we simply admired the art relics as the trophies of courageous travellers and explorers, and the whole of Africa seemed to be nothing more than a mysterious land of discoveries and explorations. This synonymous relation between fetishes, Africa and travellers now appears unbelievably naïve and primitive. We recall this state of affairs not from a desire to recall a curiosity but because the items in our art collections themselves bring to mind the times and the atmosphere which were able to embrace the fetish, explorer and the whole of Africa in a single sweep of adventurous mystery. Even the Prague collections of African art, most of which are located in the Náprstek Museum today, originated in that period. Consequently, they will always be not only the object of admiration as works of art but also a reminder of the role Czech explorers played in the discovery of Africa.

For quite some time the African continent resisted all attempts at closer study, only the narrow coastline being accessible. One of the reasons was the relative poverty of this continent, the small possibility of economic exploitation; the other was the difficulty of penetration into the interior. In the north, behind the Mediterranean coast which was known already in ancient history, there was a wide stretch of desert land, and in the equatorial zone thick jungles and fierce tribes of black Africans stood, all forboding to the adventurous spirit. As a result the southern part of the continent and some of the coastal areas were the first and most thickly to be settled by Europeans.

It was to these regions also that the pioneer Czech travellers confined themselves. As early as at the end of the Middle Ages Bohuslav Hasištejnský of Lobkovice travelled to Egypt and Tunisia in 1491; Martin Kabátník in his search for a true church of Christ arrived in Egypt in 1492. In addition there were Krištof Harant of Polžice and Bezdružice (1596) and Jindřich Matyáš Thurn (1585-1587). In the 17th and 18th centuries certain Czech missionaries went to these areas: Jakub Římař (1712-1715) and the interesting Franciscan friar Remedius Prudký who travelled to Ethiopia as the first Czech in 1751, visited the capital city of Gondar, stopped for a time in Madagascar, and returned home by ship around the continent. The Evangelical missionary Karel Augustin Pácalt (1813-1818) worked in the Hottentot settlement of Hoogekraal, Dutch South Africa which was renamed Pácaltdorp after him.

The scientific explorations, the period of great discoveries, the period of the Stanleys, Livingstones and Junkers do not begin until the 19th century. Only then do we find painstakingly and scientifically equipped explorers journeying to study the African hinterland and its peoples.

In the forefront of the Czech scientific explorers stands Dr. Emil Holub who from his own resources and indifferent public support undertook two major trips to South Africa in 1872-1879 and 1883 to 1887. On his first trip he visited and studied the territories of the BaTlapins, BaRolongs and other Bechuana tribes where he was favourably accepted as a doctor by their king in the city of Moshanengo and where he collected many valuable items for his collection. He penetrated as far north as Shoshong, capital city of the BaMangwatos, visited the salt lakes of Tsitani, Makarikari and Soa, and reached the river Zambezi and the Victoria Falls on August 9, 1875. The most important scientific acquisition from this trip was the Hottentot casts of people and animals which he picked up in the environs of Rivertown. Aside from the Náprstek Museum they considerably enriched the Vienna and London Museums.

On his second trip which he embarked on with a smaller group of associates, Dr. Holub acquired further valuable Hottentot casts and ethnographic items from the BaRotse, MaSupia, MaToko and other tribes. Approaching the village of Galulonga, north of Zambezi, he was struck with misfortune. During his absence the expedition was attacked and burnt by the MaShukulumbwes, and Dr. Holub himself only barely escaped. Despite the fact that the attack practically destroyed everything he had, Dr. Holub was still able to collect a quantity of interesting material on his return trip.

Even before Dr. Holub, the diamond hunter and world traveller Čeněk Páclt (1870) had wandered throughout Africa, visiting the same spots as Dr. Holub. He spent the rest of his life in South Africa and journeyed through Transvaal, Swazi and the Zulu country, and visited the Zambezi. He died in Cape Colony in 1887. From 1883 to 1885, E. St. Vráz explored North Africa, Upper Quincy, Gambia, Sierra Leone, Liberia and the Gold Coast. He also visited the then extant Ashanti Empire.

Dr. Antonín Stecker worked in the Sahara and Ethiopia. On his first trip (1878-1879) he accompanied the explorer F. G. Rohlfs to the Wadai sultan. His second trip was once more with Rohlfs in 1880, this time to the court of King John of Ethiopia. After Rohlfs departed from Ethiopia, Stecker continued on his own and explored Lake Tana and its surroundings.

Several expeditions to Africa were undertaken during this century and many a Czech put in his share towards building the collections of ethnographic and art items. There was, for example, the renowned scholar and linguist, Dr. Pavel Šebesta, who was concerned chiefly with a study of the pygmies in the Ituri jungles in the Congo (1929-1930). Martin Lány, who worked first as a missionary and later as a farmer in Marang at the foothills of Kilimanjaro, was responsible principally for introducing us to the tools, instruments and utensils of everyday use in the African's life.

The ethnographic and art objects, with which these explorers have built up the collections of the Náprstek Museum in Prague, never cease to be a testimony to their courage and energy even though we see them only in the quiet retreats of the institutes, studios and exhibition halls. They also tell of the courage and energy, self-confidence and capabilities of the creators themselves, whose life, philosophy, rituals and superstitions conditioned the

content and form of the relics. A certain anthropologist once called these rituals and superstitions and philosophy of the Africans "a tragic chronicle of human error and misjudgment, of unsuccessful ventures and unfulfilled expectations." But with equal right we may also say that the art objects are a chronicle of courage with which the explorers persevered despite the errors, misjudgments and failures; a chronicle of obstinate energy with which they put themselves heart and soul into new and new ventures; and a chronicle of self-confidence with which they overcame disappointment. In this sense we once again return to the intimate relationship between African art, the life of the African people and Czech explorers who devoted their lives to the study of Africa.

Václav Šolc

AFRICA—NEGRO SCULPTURES

108. Man on horseback from South Nigeria. Wood, originally decorated with red geometrical ornamentation, now black in colour. This was discovered on photographing in the ultra-violet spectrum. Height 41.2 cm., Náprstek Museum, Prague.

110. Figure of a woman from North-West Africa. Carved in stave, neck encircled with thin metal. Height 27.7 cm., Náprstek Museum, Prague (see No 118).

111. Figure of a man from North-West Africa. Carved in stave (see No 118), metal spiral at waist, height 28.5 cm., Náprstek Museum, Prague.

112. Case for Ngilingili charm. Possibly from Belgian Congo. Wood with textile and network of bark-fibre. Bean fruit on head. Height 24 cm., Náprstek Museum, Prague (see No 115).

115. Case for charm as No 112. Detail, originally some other material such as kauri shell, metal or mirror in eye sockets.

116. Figure of a man from Belgian Congo. Wood with textile and metal. Height 22,5 cm., private collection.

117. Two figures of ancestors. Possibly from Cameroons. Wood, height 33 and 31.5 cm., Náprstek Museum Prague.

118. Group of figures carved in stave from North-West Africa. Náprstek Museum, Prague, (see Nos. 110, 111).

119. Horseman from Nigeria—the Yoruba Tribe. Polychrome wood, height 44.7 cm., Náprstek Museum, Prague.

120. Man with knife from French Equatorial Africa—the Babembe Tribe. Wood with textile. Height 23.5 cm., Náprstek Museum, Prague.

121. Two figures carved in light wood from North-West Africa(?). Remnants of white paint. Height 10.7 and 11.5 cm., Náprstek Museum, Prague.

122. Figure of a woman from Sierra Leone—the Mendi Tribe. Height 49 cm., private collection.

123. Figure of a woman from Sierra Leone—the Mendi Tribe. Height 43 cm., Náprstek Museum, Prague.

124. Figure of a woman from Belgian Congo. Brown wood with copper and leather. Height 13 cm., private collection.

125. Figure of a woman, as in No 124. Detail.

126. Case for Ngilingili charm in form of human figure from Belgian Congo. Detail; wood; body originally wrapped in textile or other material, eye-sockets once inlaid. Height 14.5 cm., private collection.

117

120

121

124

Solo: THE GATES OF THE CAVE
ARE SHUT
Solo: THE GATES OF THE CAVE
ARE SHUT
Chorus: SHUT ARE THE GATES
Solo: THE SOULS OF THE DEAD ARE CROWDING THERE
IN DROVES, LIKE A SWARM OF FLIES
LIKE A SWARM OF FLIES, DANCING AT EVENING TIME
Chorus: DANCING AT EVENING TIME
Solo: A SWARM OF FLIES DANCING AT EVENING TIME
WHEN THE NIGHT HAS GROWN DARK
WHEN THE SUN HAS VANISHED
WHEN THE NIGHT HAS GROWN DARK
A SWARM OF FLIES
THE WHIRLING OF DEAD LEAVES
IN A HOWLING TEMPEST
Chorus: IN A HOWLING TEMPEST
Solo: AWAITING HIM WHO WILL COME
Chorus: HIM WHO WILL COME
Solo: WHO WILL SAY
TO THIS ONE "COME" AND TO THE OTHER "GO"
Chorus: TO THIS ONE "COME" AND TO THE OTHER "GO"
Solo: AND KMVUM WILL BE WITH HIS CHILDREN
Chorus: WITH HIS CHILDREN
All: AND THAT IS THE END!

Pygmies, Equatorial Africa.

America

The Archaic Art

ARCHAIC MEXICAN ART

The term archaic art in Mexico commonly refers to all the artefacts occurring before the appearance of the Spaniards in 1519. A precise dating of these works is impossible, that is, provided they are not affixed with the hieroglyphic chronology which is quite frequently the case with the Mayan relics. In the remaining works we are limited to inferences, being guided by the site of discovery, technique of workmanship and kinship to one or the other national style. On the whole, it may be said that the majority of art relics, including the works illustrated in this book, were produced between A. D. 1 and 1519, in other words, over a period of 15 centuries.

The oldest relics are the figurines of the so-called archaic horizontal; according to some archeologists they were produced some considerable time before the birth of Christ. These archaic figurines of fired clay almost exclusively represent women with prominently emphasized hips as the symbol of fertility. Similar figurines may be found throughout the entire breadth of the country, a fact which possibly suggests the simultaneous settlement of the gigantic country by wandering tribes of primitive Indians living off game and wild fruits.

The decisive factor, which transformed the character of the entire culture and led to far-reaching differentiation in regions and nations, was the discovery of agriculture. Some four to five thousand years ago the Mayan aborigines first succeeded in cultivating maize on the territory of present-day Guatemala. The plant was taken over by the other tribes and in time, aided by the existence of a common economy, became the principal source of human nutrition. The wealth of the humble maize made possible an unprecedented growth of the population (before the Spaniards came there were nine million people living in ancient Mexico), the flowering of large cities, and the tremendous development of art and science.

The Mayans probably advanced the furthest, and it seems that neither their scientific nor their artistic achievements have been surpassed by any other nation of Mexico. They created the most perfect system of writing in America and the best system of numbers in the world for that period (the discovery of zero and the positional significance of numerals in the twenty system). Their calendar, more exact than anything Europe had to offer then, the organization of their society, the unbelievable accomplishments in monumental constructions are just as significant as their mastery of art forms in sculpture, architecture and painting.

The character of this book precludes the reproduction of other than sculptural relics and of these only those which found their way into Czechoslovak collections. It just happens that the branches of Mayan art which are dealt with in this book are the least impressive, for the most distinctive feature is to be found particularly in the monuments (stelæ), temple constructions and mural paintings. The small Mayan works were less preserved, relatively speaking, than other Mexican relics. Only one Mayan figure is found in our book, the product of a provincial region (Yaina Island) where similar figurines were produced from forms (both the form and cast are of fired clay).

While the home of the Mayas was the mountains and forests of Guatemala, Honduras and the Mexican states of Chiapas, Tabasco and Yucatan, other important cultural centres arose elsewhere in Mexico. The Toltec culture crystallized in the heart of the country in the plateaux, culminating sometime in the sixth century. Its most beautiful pyramids and relics are still standing today in the giant dead city of Teotihuacan, 40 km. to the north of the present day capital. Typical for their severely religious and hieratically rigid style are the broad, enigmatically smiling faces. These together with the pyramids tempt the inexperienced student to think erroneously that he is dealing with an art derived from Egypt. Similarly unfounded hypotheses identified Mayan art from Quirigua with the art relics of India, or from the Mayan city of Palenque with China. Today it is hardly necessary to emphasize that the art of the American Indians had its own peculiar history. A distinct, independent art grew up on new soil under different conditions from the rudiments that were brought over from Asia by Mongoloid stocks some ten to fifteen thousand years ago. Interestingly, the theory on the Mongoloid origin of the Indians is the product of the last century, the work of our great countryman, the anthropologist Aleš Hrdlička. Even up to the 19th century the dominant theory was the religious teaching that the Indians were the descendants of the ten lost tribes of Israel, a teaching that only served to perpetuate the biblical story of the sons of Ham, Shem and Japheth peopling the world.

From the latest epoch of Toltec art come figurines in which the austerity of forms is lost under the welter of vestments. A kindred culture arose in Cholule where among other things the largest pyramid in the world was preserved (the Spaniards built a large Catholic church on the top). A characteristic relic from this site is a small fife in the shape of a monkey's head.

In the magnificent culture of the Zapotecs in south Mexico we also come across broad faces similar to the Toltec. Many of the clay urns were gathered up for archeological collections.

The relics from Colima and Nayarit on the Pacific coast assume a special status in the marginal but nonetheless important arts. They are the least restrained by the "high" hieratic style and resemble most likely what we call folk art. There occur elements that are purposely comical and contorted into motions, and unusually ingenious forms of fifes. Some of the plastics strongly resemble primitive African art.

The Aztecs were the very last to enter the scene of ancient Mexican history. A few centuries before the Spaniards, they swept down the plains of Mexico like barbarians, subjugated in the course of time all the nations extant in that period, partly absorbed their cultures and finally created a unique monumental art.

Norbert Frýd

130. Seal from Mexico. Fired clay. The seal was used to imprint decorations on the body. Anthropomorphic figure in the centre and two-headed snakes on both sides. 6 × 7 cm., Náprstek Museum, Prague.

135. Little head from Mexico. Fired clay. Height 4 cm., Náprstek Museum, Prague.

137. Votive figure from Mexico. Fired clay, fragment, central height 11 cm., Náprstek Museum, Prague.

138. Little head from Mexico. Coarse-grained stone, height 2.4 cm., private collection.

139. Torso from Mexico—Atscapotzalco. Fired clay, archaic period, height 9 cm., private collection.

140. Figurine of a woman from Mexico. Fired clay, archaic period, height 8.2 cm., private collection.

141. Figurine of a woman from Mexixo. Fired clay, archaic period, height 9 cm., private collection.

142. Two women figurines from Mexico—Tlatilco. Fired clay, remnants of polychromy, e. g. red on the hair. The so-called archaic horizontal, produced before the birth of Christ, symbol of fertility with marked emphasis of the hips and mask-like setting of the little faces. Height 14 and 11.5 cm., private collection.

143. Two figures of men from Mexico—Colima. Brown fired clay with incised streaks and black drawing. Height 23 and 15.5 cm., private collection.

144. Head of a monkey(?) Fired clay. Mexico, height 6,5 cm. Náprstek Museum, Prague.

145. Fife in the shape of a monkey's head from Mexico—Cholula. Fired clay, by covering the opening on the right side of the face the sound can be lowered by one tone. Height 7 cm., private collection.

146. Two votive figurines from Mexico—Teotihuacan. Figures of women in ceremonial dress, grey fired clay, imprints from form, Toltec culture. One of them, 12 cm. high, has a four-edged veil, one corner of which falls to the front (the so-called kechkemetl worn by some Mexican women even today); the round ear-rings are of obsidian and the rosettes on the diadem of coloured corn paper. The child is carried on the hips in the Indian manner, "hekmek." The rear figurine is 8 cm. tall. Private collection.

147. Figure of a priest from Mexico—Yaina Island. Fired clay, made from form, within the sphere of the Mayan Empire. Height 12 cm., Náprstek Museum, Prague.

148. Ceremonial flute. Clay pressed into a form, remnants of white paint. Toiomac culture. Height 19,8 cm., private collection.

149. Urn in the shape of a seated man from Mexico—Oaxaca. Grey fired clay, remnants of polychromy, Zapotec culture, height 18.6 cm., private collection (see No 150).

150. Urn in the shape of a seated man, as No 149, *en face*.

151. Urn in the shape of a seated woman from Mexico—Oaxaca. Grey fired clay, Zapotec culture. The woman is dressed similarly as the Toltec figurine described in No 146 and has filed teeth. Height 16.6 cm., private collection.

152. Head of Chipi, deity of Death and Rebirth. Fired clay, fragment of a vessel(?). Zapotec culture, height 12 cm., width 12 cm., private collection.

153. Spout of a vessel from Mexico—Teotihuacan. Fragment of a vessel with decoration on the neck. The mask is an imprint from a form. Fired clay, Toltec culture, height 12.5 cm., private collection.

154. Head of Chipi, as No 152, profile.

155. Child with a ball from Mexico. Red fired clay, polychromy, Zapotec culture, height 27 cm., private collection.

156. Head of a vessel in the shape of a seated man from Mexico—Nayarit. Grey fired clay, height of the entire vessel 29 cm., the visible part 10 cm., private collection (see No 157).

157. Head of a vessel in the shape of a seated man. *En face* of same head as in No 156.

158. Head of a strangled man from Mexico. Fired clay, height 6 cm., Náprstek Museum, Prague.

159. Head of a priest from Mexico. Fired clay, height 35 cm., Náprstek Museum, Prague.

160. Seated figures of a man and woman from Mexico—Colima. Fired clay, height 9 and 10 cm., private collection.

161. Figure of a woman(?) from Mexico. Malachite, height 6 cm., Náprstek Museum, Prague.

162. Seated man with an animal's head from Mexico. Stone of volcanic origin, Aztec culture, height 12 cm., Náprstek Museum, Prague (see No 163).

163. Seated man with an animal's head, as in No 162.

164. Tlaloc—the God of Rain from Central America. Stone probably of volcanic origin, height 18 cm., private collection.

165. Human figure from Mexico. Porous stone, height 23 cm., Náprstek Museum, Prague.

166. Punch from Columbia. Three-edged red-brown stone for punching metal leaves. On the three surfaces are stylized figures of a man, woman and child. Prehistoric period, height 7.5 cm., private collection (see No 167).

167. Punch, as in No 166.

168. Sacrificial bowl(?) from Columbia. In form of a human head, black stone, height 4.4 cm., private collection.

140

144

148

151

157

158

159

162

HERE IT MUST NOW BE TOLD HOW ONCE THE WORLD WAS FLOATING IN PROFOUND SILENCE, IN PROFOUND PEACE, HOW IT REMAINED AT PEACE AND GENTLY ROCKED, HOW IT LAY WASTE AND WAS EMPTY.

AND THIS IS THE FIRST REPORT AND THE FIRST TESTIMONY: THERE WAS NEITHER MAN NOR BEAST, NOR BIRD, FISH, CRAB, TREE, STONE, CAVE, ROCK, GRASS NOR BUSH – ONLY THE SKY WAS THERE.

THE FACE OF THE EARTH WAS INVISIBLE, ONLY THE SEA WAS SWELLING UNDER THE VAULTED SKY AND THAT WAS ALL...

ONLY THE BUILDER AND THE CREATOR, THE POWERFUL ONE AND CUCUMATZ, THE MOTHER AND THE GENITOR WERE PRESENT IN THE WATERS INFINITE. YES, THEY WERE WRAPPED IN GREEN AND BLUE FEATHERS; AND THIS NAME "THE PLUMED SERPENT" WAS GIVEN THEM, AND BY NATURE THEY WERE ALL PERCEIVING AND ALL KNOWING.

ALSO THE SKY WAS TRULY THERE AND THE "HEART OF THE SKY" WAS THERE, THAT IS THE NAME OF GOD, THAT'S HOW HE IS CALLED.

AND HIS WORD REACHED THEM, IT CAME TO THE POWERFUL ONE AND TO CUCUMATZ, THERE INTO THE DARKNESS AND NIGHT AND IT SPOKE TO THE POWERFUL ONE AND TO CUCUMATZ. AND THEY SPOKE AND TOOK COUNSEL, THEY MEDITATED WITH CARE, THEY COMMUNICATED AND ACCORDED THEIR WORDS AND THEIR THOUGHTS.

AND THERE CAME ABOUT THE FIRST BEGINNING OF LIGHT, THERE MAN APPEARED IN THEIR INTENTIONS.

From the Indian manuscript Popol Vuh, summarizing
the oral tradition of the Quiché tribe (Guatemala).

America

Haida, Tlinkit, Kwakiutl

172

THE ART OF THE INDIANS
FROM THE NORTH-WEST COAST

Very little and sometimes practically nothing is known of the origin and period of development of Indian culture. All scholars today agree that the Indians probably came to America from the Mongolian plains. But whether they brought with them the first expressions of their national fantasy or whether it was only in the new settlements that the environment, countryside and day-to-day work provoked attempts at creative artistic expression, will perhaps be determined sometime by the archeologists. All the preserved cultures of both the Americas have common features so that one can speak of an Indian culture, Indian life and expressive style. The particular development of the tribes or group of tribes is then divided into cultural entities from the prairies or mountains, town or tents, fishermen from the coast or hunters from the interior. In the course of the history of the American continent many mature and famous cultures, empires and national entities grew up, reached their peak and fell into decay; such were the empires of the Incas, Mayas, Aztecs, etc. In North America, it seems, cultural development came to a standstill at its very beginning. The most compact and most outstanding was the artistic culture of the north-western coastal tribes. We do not know when it started and can only guess when it reached its peak, but we know for certain when it was discovered.

When Juan Rodriguez Cabrillo (1542) and Sir Francis Drake (1572) sailed north along the western coast of America they were probably the first to come into contact with the Indians. But the first ships which anchored in the north-west region of the Indians and started to barter with the natives were the Russian ships of Vitus Bering and Petr Chirikov. This was in 1741. From that time on Russian expeditions often returned to this territory where they founded a barter station on the island of Kadiak and in 1799 the harbour and town of Sitka. From 1799 to 1802 as many as 48,000 otter, bear and seal skins and furs were carried away from here. Meanwhile Spanish ships had sailed several times to the coast and claimed the territory for the Spanish crown. These ships were captained by Juan Pérez, Bruno de Hazeta and Juan Francisco Bodega y Quadra. In 1778 the research expedition of James Cook landed here and brought back the first art relics, which are today in the British Museum in London. In the first half of the 19th century the first capitalist companies rushed to Indian territory and became its masters, capturing the trade and bringing civilization and "white misery" to the land of the Indians. These were the North-West Company which founded Astoria in 1814 and the Hudson Bay Company which had three trading stations here in 1835. Practically nothing remains today of Indian culture, and the Indian tribes, decimated by small-pox and syphilis brought by the Spaniards in the seventies of the 18th century, are gradually dying out. They either live a penurious life in the Canadian reservations or work in the salmon canneries in the towns for meagre wages.

The reports brought back by explorers about this coastal area and its native population, however, bear witness to the fact that powerful tribes numbering over 60,000 members once lived on the narrow coastal strip interspersed with fiords from Yakuta Bay in Alaska to the river-basin of Columbia River in Oregon, and the nearby islands under the peaks of high mountains in the east. The tribe of Haidan Indians alone numbered tens of thousands of members of which not even 1000 remain today. The most northerly of the tribes was the Thlinkitan tribe, then came the Tsimshian, Haidan, Bellacoola, Kwakiutl and Nutka tribes and finally, in the southernmost part of this unified cultural region were the Salishes of the seaboard. The Haidan tribe lived on the island of Queen Charlotte. The Kwakiutl, Nutka and partly also the Salishan tribes lived on Vancouver Island.

The first description of the artistic expressions of the Indians of the Haidan tribe come from the book "Voyage autour du Monde, pendant les années 1790, 1791 et 1792" by Etienne Marchand. He writes about the house totem as follows: "An entrance hole is cut out in a strong tree trunk of great girth which rears up in the centre above the dwelling. It has the appearance of a human mouth, or rather animal jaws, over which there protrudes a hooked beak about two feet long, corresponding in its dimensions to a monstrous face . . . and above this rises the gigantic figure of an erect man which forms the end of the sculptural decoration of the front; the head of the statue is covered with a hat in the form of a loaf of sugar, as high as the figure itself. In those places where there are no main figures the surface of the trunk is carved with likenesses of frogs, toads, lizards and other animals . . ."

Other reliable reports come from 1779 and 1785 when the French explorers Comte de la Pérouse and Francisco Mourelle described the colours and texture of the Shilkat blankets of the Thlinkitan tribe, an analogy to which is found only in the peak cultural period of Peruan textile art. The most accurate proofs are, of course, the photographs, which run into hundreds, taken in the villages of the north-western coastal Indians by R. Maynard from Victoria in British Columbia.

James Cook (1778), Alejandro Malaspina (1792) and Captain George Vancouver (1793-1794) testify that they saw totems on the coast. James Cook adds that in 1778 all the Indians he met had metal instruments and knives which probably contributed to the development of wood-carving.

It is certain that at the turn of the 18th century the sculptural and artistic work of the coastal Indians was flourishing and probably at its height.

Originally—as is proved by excavations about 3000 years old discovered on the Frazer River—the sculptural expressions of the Indians were hewn from stone. Their style undoubtedly continued, at least in their fundamental features, in the wood-carvings of the 18th century. The connection here goes back a long way. The main and most well-known artistic expression of the coastal Indians were totems, always turned towards the sea. These were either huge memorials reaching up to twenty metres, small grave totems, house totems set up above the facade, or supporting pillars, or totems denoting the place of honour inside the dwelling. Canoes, boxes and coffins from cedar planks, steamed, bent and joined together, and finally utensils and masks are all decorated with carved and painted patterns having an animal theme or ornamental content.

The Indians along the Pacific coast lived mostly by fishing. They caught whales and salmon, or collected shells, mussels, edible seaweed and other sea products. They added tobacco to shells ground with putty in a mortar and chewed it. Pipes were not known to them. In addition to fishing, they ensured their daily food by hunting game and wild goats and collecting wild fruit and herbs, all of which provided them with subjects for artistic portrayal. In sculpture, reliefs and ornamental decoration they always returned in their themes of sea-monsters, sperm-whales, whales, sea-lions, octopuses, sharks, frogs, bears, wolves, beavers, double-headed snakes, eagles, ravens, vultures, elks and reindeer.

Sculpture, carving and painting were the arts of the men, while the women wove, knitted and did basket-work. Wood and bark of all kinds were practically the only artistic materials.

The relation between content and form can be seen in the artistic expressions of the Indians in the same way as in any other mature artistic expression. Art must always be appreciated as any other social phenomenon—in its historical context.

It is typical for the primitive life of certainly unprofessional artists that all artistic expressions have an idea-content and depict known reality in a naturally abbreviated form. With the Indian artists this abbreviation is nearly always very compact, simple and borders on monumentality. The individual workmanship of the wood-carver is of course on a level with his technical ability and power of imagination.

All the artistic features of Indian art are comprehensible. This of course does not mean that they are always as intelligible to us as to the Indians who know the subject from their daily life. What may seem incomprehensible abstractions to us is comprehensible to the Indian spectator at first glance. He knows nature and has the same experiences as the artist.

There is thus nothing unrealistic in it for the Indian spectator if the artist from the depths of his knowledge depicts not only what he sees but all that goes into the subject. For example, he may depict not only the shape, outline and surface of a whale or bird but also its backbone and innards.

A substantial role in the art of the coastal Indians is played by symbols arising out of the social system, legends and myths, religion and superstition, and their views on natural and supernatural phenomena. The totem is regarded with the greatest esteem in every family. Each tribe or clan has its totem animals. In every family and according to laws on heredity the sanctity of the name is inviolable and it may not be stolen on pain of sanguinary retribution. Nature is ruled by immortal spirits residing in people, animals and trees. The heroes of mythology are animals. On the Aleutian Islands this is the griffin-vulture, while the coastal Indians have mainly the raven, which despite its solemnity and the Promethean myth that it stole the sun from the home of supernatural beings and broke it into a thousand pieces which gave rise to the stars, bears all the realistic and comic features of the raven.

The mask is an indispensable part of dance rituals and the magic of the shamans. The shaman or medicine man, sorcerer or magician of the tribe, distinguished himself from the superstitious crowd of nobles, freemen and slaves chiefly by his ability to think up deceptive tricks and freaks by which he roused the wonder of the spectators in surroundings particularly suitable for such things, e.g. around a fire in a dark house. He actually deluded the public with coffins having a double bottom and puppets and objects secreted in the cavity of the mouth, just as magicians do now. In this he was aided by fear and horror—fear of supernatural phenomena and the horror of masks having expressions of death, pain, terror, ironical and wicked smiles. With each mask he donned, the actor was invaded by the spirit of that mask. Such was the case with the whistler mask—the spirit of forest blizzards—with lips pursed for whistling, the clapper mask with continually clapping lips, or the bird mask which revealed another, fearfully painted, black human mask inside when it opened wide its wooden beak. The masks were usually larger than a human head in size. In Indian art the head is always bigger than that corresponding to the natural proportions of the body and head. The eyes and eyebrows are standardized in masks as well as in all artistic expressions.

The dances of masked Indians usually took place in the winter months on the occasion of great festivals known as "potlatch." This word, which comes from the Indian tribe of Nutka where it means "gift", passed into the Chinookan jargon, the language used by all Indians in inter-tribal dealings. These festivals were held so that the chiefs of families could boast of their wealth, enhance their social standing and glorify the sound of their name. Here they could also humble their enemies for those who received gifts had to repay them in the same value at the earliest opportunity. This property-bragging extended sometimes to the ruin and plundering of their property by the giving away of everything so that all their enemy donors should be shamed and humbled. It is natural that the masks for these occasions were not affable and smiling.

As regards artistic influences, these became almost indistinguishable among the Indian tribes on the coast. The Tsimshian tribe accepted some motifs such as flowers and leaves from the Athapascans of the interior. The Thlinkitans, neighbouring with the Eskimos in the north, decorated their masks with small faces. But only with the coastal Salishes, who were outstanding seafarers, is the conjecture possible that on their travels they took over some Asiatic traits of style. The Indians accepted no artistic influences from the Europeans. The Art Museum in Denver (Colorado, U.S.A.), contains the only known mask with a realistic face of a white man, which recalls Abraham Lincoln, and in the Museum in Victoria there is a statue—a sewing machine.

The sharp colours peculiar to northern peoples have a narrow scale—red, black, yellow, greenish-blue and white. The Indians ground the colours obtained from moulds, berries, charcoal, ochre and copper in a mortar. They obtained the characteristic greenish-blue from copper soaked in urine, and red from salmon roes. Their diluting agent was naturally oil or some kind of fish oil. The morphological alphabet of expression is flat and linear, the outlines are drawn with a thick black line. Sometimes part of a picture is enclosed in a thick frame, thus achieving greater prominence. Inspite of the fact that cold colours are used nearly everywhere their effect is on the whole warm.

The forms and even the angles are rounded off. The circle, ellipse and rounded-off rectangle are repeated in sculptural works by a sphere or egg-shaped, concave or convex forms. The ornament always follows the form logically and is composed to harmonize with it. The most frequent form of all is the eye—an eye as such, an eye as a joint, as the

centre of another form, as a navel or as the filling to empty surfaces. Indian artists could not stand empty surfaces and were unable to mould them into space. An understanding of space and its representation were lacking.

From the transformation and abbreviation of form of some idea-content, usually extremely concrete, the rhythmical picture was transposed into a pattern. For example a fish was joined either by the tail-fin or mouth and repeated on the decorated surface one or more times. Halved faces or a simultaneous view of three sides was rather a question of a base for ornamentation than an incorrect understanding of perspective.

It has a deep expression, the portrayal of passion, anger, wickedness or power expressed not only in human but also in birds' faces. The mask always expresses some emotion of thought, intention or character. It is a functional art; rarely is there a statue for a statue's sake. It is either a mask, rattle, grave-stone, box, spade, ladle or button. There are, or were, few objects of daily use which were not decorated. The art of the coastal Indian tribes from the north-west sea-board of Alaska, Canada and Oregon (U.S.A.) is an art with a mature national form of an old, truly American culture.

Lost as a result of the disregard of the commercial civilizers for Indian art, scattered throughout private collections, Indian art is now the object of the interest of cultural institutions and research workers—an interest shown almost too late. Today science must reconstruct the glorious culture of the past from mere fragments. The plates in this book must carry out the task of acquainting the reader with those Indian works of art which are to be found in Czechoslovakia and which deserve closer acquaintance.

Adolf Hoffmeister

AMERICA: HAIDA, TLINKIT
AND KWAKIUTL

172. Mask of the God of the Winds from the Haida Tribe Wood. The eyelashes were at one time decorated with hair but in the present state are simply bare skin. Height 38 cm., private collection (see No 182).

174. Canoe with hunters from the Haida Tribe. Wood, sparsely painted, length 37 cm, Náprstek Museum, Prague.

176. Two miniature totems from the Tlinkit Tribe. Slate, height 18 and 21 cm., State Castle of Opočno.

178. Miniature totem from the Haida Tribe. Painted wood, height 21 cm., Náprstek Museum, Prague.

181. Ceremonial mask from the Tlinkit Tribe. Wood, polychromy, height 19 cm., private collection.

182. Two masks from the Haida and Kwakiutl Tribes. The left: see No 172. The right: hard wood, movable tongue. Height 38 and 27 cm., private collection.

184. Bowl in shape of two animals from the Haida Tribe. Wood, length 30 cm., State Castle of Opočno.

186. Bast mat from the Kwakiutl Tribe. Decorated with a drawing in black, red and green depicting in totem style animal forms on the sides and a human figure in the middle. Dimensions 110 cm. by 95 cm. Náprstek Museum, Prague.

188. Bast hat from the Kwakiutl Tribe. Drawing in black, red and green depicting *en face* a face without nose and with a widely opened mouth. Diameter 23 cm., Náprstek Museum, Prague.

189. Hat, as no No 188, profile.

190. Miniature totem from Tlinkit Tribe. Slate, height 35 cm., State Castle of Opočno.

191. Miniature totem, detail of No 190.

192. Two figures from the Haida Tribe. Wood, brightly coloured, red-brown decoration in bast. Height 68 and 43 cm., Náprstek Museum, Prague.

193. Vessel with a face from the Haida Tribe. Narrower side of a rectangular wooden vessel. Height 8 cm., Náprstek Museum, Prague.

194. Spoon carved of brown goat's horn, from the Haida Tribe. The eyes of the animal are in-laid with mother-of-pearl. Length 24 cm., private collection.

IN LARGE
EVER LARGER CIRCLES
THE SHADOW OF THE BIRD KAWA CREEPS ALONG
ACROSS THE RAPIDS, THROUGH THE PLACE
OF MY PASSING
I LOOK
I LOOK UP TO HIM
AND KAWA SHOUTS DOWN TO ME
AND WITH A STROKE OF THE WING
TURNS TO FLY AWAY.

IN LARGE
EVER LARGER CIRCLES
THE EAGLE FLIES AROUND THE TREE
THE EAGLE FLIES ABOVE HIS NEST
WATCHING.

HE SHOUTS
HIS SHOUT FLIES
IT SOUNDS AFAR
ALL THROUGH THE LAND, THE ENEMY
WARNING.

Song of the Pawnee Indians, North America.

Oceania

THE ART OF OCEANIA

P. M. Boule, Paul Rivet and other scientists in the cultural field, the content, importance and magnitude of whose works we are realizing only now, have reached the conclusion that at some date in the miocene and pliocene periods such a sudden development of man occurred along the coast of the Indian and Pacific Oceans, in a region abounding in favourable natural conditions, that several different types appeared simultaneously. This also explains the heterogeneous culture and anthropology and similarity in language of the enormous number of national and tribal entities.

Of interest to us in this study are the artistic expressions of the inhabitants of the Pacific island region which is usually termed the art of the South Seas or Oceanic art. This region, which also includes Australia and some island tribes of Indonesia (such as the Dayaks in Borneo), is more correctly divided into three groups, Polynesia, Melanesia and Micronesia, where—undisturbed by external influences and encouraged by frequent inter-island relations—there grew up distinct cultures from a common basis and preserving outstanding features.

Polynesia includes the Fiji Islands (Vanua Levu, Viti Levu); Samoa, Tonga, Tahiti, Rarotonga; Hervey, Society and Cook Islands; Marquesas (Nuka-Hiva, Uahuka, Uapu, Hivaova, Fatuhiva); Easter Islands (Tekan-hangaoaru or Rapa-Nui); New Zealand, the Hawaiian or Sandwich Islands (Hawaii, Maui, Molokai, Oahu and Kauai).

Melanesia comprises the New Caledonian Islands (Uvea, Mare and Lifu) and the Loyalty Islands; the New Hebrides (Malekula and Ambrym); New Guinea and its intrinsic regions (Dutch New Guinea, the Sepik river basin, the Huon Gulf region, Massine region, Trobrian Islands, the Papua region, the Torres Strait region; New Britain with the Gazeli peninsula and the New Ireland Islands; the Admiralty Islands (Pak, Lou and Baluan); the Solomon Islands (Buka, Bird Island, Bougainville, Choiseul, Vella Lavella, New Georgia, Santa Isabel, Malaita, Ulava, Guadalcanar, San Cristobal, Rennel).

Micronesia includes the Marianas, Caroline, Marshall and Gilbert Islands.

When Pope Alexander VI divided the world between the Portuguese and Spanish, the former received the east and the latter the west. Thus when the Spanish King Charles V refused the Portuguese the right to the most easterly of their island bases—the Moluccas—he sent a fleet under the command of the Portuguese renegade Magellan to secure it for the Spanish crown, quite in the spirit of the Papal bull—in the west. Thus it happened that Magellan unwittingly discovered the Pacific Ocean and was the first to land on the Mariana Islands after wandering across the Pacific suffering terribly from hunger and thirst. He himself died somewhere in the Philippines (1521) and of his entire fleet only one ship, the Victoria, returned with eighteen men and Captain Sebastian de Cano, who was the first person not only to travel round the world but also to discover the Oceanic island region.

The Hidalgos from South and Central America, Mexico and Peru, discovered a number of Oceanic islands in the sixteenth century but owing to the insufficient mapping and measuring abilities of the crew the discoveries

were lost and later explorers with full justification discovered them anew. Thus, for example, Alvaro de Mendana started out from Callao-Lima and in 1568 discovered the Solomon Islands but in another expedition in 1595 he was unable to find them again. The Solomon Islands were discovered once more two centuries later. New Guinea was discovered simultaneously by the Portuguese from the east and the Spaniards from the west.

Sir Francis Drake, William Dampier and other seafarers of England and Holland, such as Van Schouten, ploughed the Pacific Ocean in the second half of the 16th and in the 17th centuries, more out of hatred for the Spanish aggressors than with the intention of making discoveries. The Dutchman Roggevein discovered the Easter Islands in 1722. Nowhere did the white men behave well. They looted and murdered without reason. But the worst terror of the Pacific Ocean were the Peruvian slavers who, for example, carried off practically the whole population of the Easter Islands, including the king, for slave work in collecting guano.

The second half of the 18th century saw a struggle for power over the Pacific Ocean between the British and French. Wallis discovered Tahiti (1767), Bougainville the New Hebrides, etc.

But it is to James Cook and Admiral Comte de La Pérouse with their discoveries that we are indebted for a knowledge of what up to that time was an unknown corner of the world.

James Cook was the first to determine the homogeneousness of the inhabitants of the enormous Oceanic-Australian region. He not only discovered but also really explored New Caledonia, the New Hebrides, Eastern Australia, New Zealand, Polynesia, Tahiti, Tonga, Marquesas, Hawaii and the Cook Islands and although he did not discover the Antarctic, at least he anticipated it. Comte de La Pérouse, that generous and magnanimous sailor, carried on and completed Cook's researches. It was to him that Louis XVI gave the order to deal with the natives "with great care and humanity and to acquaint them with France only through benevolent and generous deeds."

In the 19th century expedition followed expedition, most of them English and French. From 1803 to 1821 there were three large Russian expeditions. On the deck of the ship "Beagle" we see the great materialist scientist Darwin, the American Melville and the Englishman Stevenson who were the first of a number of cultural explorers, novelists and artists such as later Paul Gauguin, Pierre Loti, Joseph Conrad, Jack London, Victor Seqalen, Marc Chadourne and Alain Gerbault. Poetic descriptions of the journeys of great writers can be found in the charming book "Susan and the Pacific Ocean" by Jean Giraudoux, in the tales of colonizers by Somerset Maugham, and in the misanthropic "Book of a Refugee from the Lands of People" by D. H. Lawrence who was the first to discover in the spiritual and artistic expression of the Oceanic natives those deep relations with the monumentality of nature which he had found only in the lands of the Celts.

Denis Diderot was the first to attempt to penetrate philosophically into the spiritual region of the Oceanic peoples and their cultures. In his famous treatise "Supplément au Voyage de Bougainville" he eloquently and frequently also sentimentally described the Oceanic savages as the prototype of the primitive man. This French conception of a "good man" unspoilt by civilization and living in the "golden age" of humanity on the "Fortune Islands" can be traced from Montaigne through Jean Jacques Rousseau and Denis Diderot to the romantics of the 19th century. Without a real scientific cognition of the Oceanic regions the application of these philosophical conclusions thus appears as a quite unreal, idealistic disembodiment.

Melville came the nearest to a cognition of the cultural bases and creative impulses of the Oceanic natives during his four-year sojourn on the Marquesas Islands with the Taipi cannibals in the valley of Nuka-Hiva Island. Here he recognized that their way of life was as importantly different and equally justified as the way of the west. In 1840, together with Dumont d'Urville, he participated in the taking of Tahiti for France and learnt to know perfectly the beautiful terror and terrible beauty of the mysteries of the Pacific.

Robert Louis Stevenson, a Scot, whom the Samoan natives solemnly buried on the mountain of Vea in 1895, was not merely looking for treasure islands but also raised his voice against the racketeering and plundering by the whites in his "Letters from the Southern Seas" and "Codicil to History."

In dealing with Oceanic research one must bear in mind, as they did, that this is a different culture from ours, from another human era than our contemporary one, another mental region than ours; cultural modesty is necessary for every real cognition.

The art of Polynesia bears the marks of some old artistic experiences and a feeling for artistic order. The population, which probably came from Indonesia around 1000 in the first wave of migration, is darker and hardier. The immigrants of Malayan origin came in the second wave of the migration of nations (about the 13th and 14th centuries) across Melanesia, bringing with them a certain amount of learning and a knowledge of the great Asiatic cultures, and mixed with the aborigines. From this union there arose a culture of artistic crafts and the first expressions of artistic feeling; a religion appeared at the same time, which was an expression of the eternal strife between *mana* and *tapu* (mana—supernatural, communicative but destroyable power; tapu—our taboo—a dangerous, harmful quality, threatening them or even their own manu). The gods of the crafts and the gods of kindred unions or ancestors were worshipped. Each clan kept careful records of its genealogy and jealously guarded family traditions. The first-born son took his father's place on the day he was born and until he came of age his father ruled the family in his name as a regent.

The Polynesians of the central islands were famous as seafarers by which means their culture spread; they migrated across the open sea to such distant island regions as the Hawaiian Islands, the Easter Islands and New Zealand.

In art the Polynesians from the central islands showed a distinct sense for symmetry, stylization and pattern. Statuettes rarely appeared. The Tahitians did not even consider the portrayal of human faces as a suitable subject. On the Cook Islands, which today bear the name of their discoverer, the inhabitants worshipped tools such as the axe, oar, spear, etc. James Cook himself named the islands the Friendly Islands, little suspecting that the Tonga tribe was preparing to attack his ship and kill him if he had not unexpectedly left a day or two earlier. And none of the friendly islanders informed him. Such was their military discipline.

All the objects of daily use bear witness to a remarkable skill and mature sense of form and purpose. A strict, repeated geometrical pattern can always be found on ritual instruments, ceremonial objects, weapons, oars, ships and textiles.

The Marquesas Islands, the nearest to the equator, are uninviting, fissured and impassable, afflicted with periodic droughts and harvest failures, hunger and thirst. The law of the first-born was kept to so strictly here that the entire property of the family passed to the first born on his coming of age. No motherly care was devoted to girls so that they often died during childhood. There were disproportionately more men than women. When the first-born married he took his brothers to live with him who, according to the law, had an equal claim to his wife.

Tattooing stood out in artistic expression. The most decorated objects were weapons, for the tribes were constantly at war. Blood-feud was a law. Religion was a family matter and live sacrifices were offered to the gods.

Since women had a subordinate position in society their artistic work was in no way outstanding. The men, however, were excellent builders and the buildings were laboriously decorated with patterns in which, in contrast to Tahitian art, human figures or faces were often repeated. Their taste for the richness of relief patterns connects the artistic feelings of the inhabitants of the Marquesas with the artistic expressions of the Maori nation in New Zealand. Jewels, hair-dress and clothing enhanced the ceremonial appearance of stone and wooden statues.

Particular attention should be paid to the Easter Islands which were famous for their stone colossi on the coast. On the slopes of the volcanoes of Pakeop, Ah and Ranorarak the aborigines of the islands hewed blocks of lava weighing up to four tons into gigantic faces, possibly to drive away their enemies. Present-day inhabitants no longer know the exact reason for the statues nor the manner in which the stones were transported from the craters to the shore. It was a monumental art.

The most outstanding artistically—on an island where there are no trees—are the smooth, realistic statuettes which were carved skilfully and with a rare sense of economy in the use of each bit of wood (mostly floated down). Since wood was a rarity these wooden ornaments were a sign of wealth of the owners who decorated themselves with them on festive occasions. The figures of men with ribbed hooked noses and whiskers were worked up sculpturally and had a strange dignity. The female figures were flat. Some statuettes of men had a bird's head in honour of the bird-god called Manutara, Make-make, who annually entered into the body of a particularly worthy member of the tribe, Tangata manu. Birds' eggs were the main food of the islanders. With the decline of the population both the taste and demand for art decreased and of all the plundered and destroyed works of art there remain only a few in the world today. The statue of the bird-man appears in four collections—in Leningrad, New York and London and in the collection of Pierre Loti in France. Even the statuettes of male figures are exceedingly rare and do not number even a hundred.

An exceptional and unique survival in the whole of Oceania are written tablets with a pictorial writing not yet deciphered, which were probably some kind of pictographic notes for priests when reciting old legends and songs—kohou—rongo—rongo. They were probably the beginnings of some ancient writing.

The Easter Islands, which have now been carefully explored scientifically, could probably still show the existence of an older culture than that discovered by Europeans. The history of the islands itself records a long list of hereditary kings with Hoatu-Matua and Tumaheke at the top, who led the tribe here from some unknown place. Experts on the Easter Islands argue on the basis of similarities in language as to whether they came from Indonesia or from elsewhere.

New Zealand, the realm of the Maori nation, is the home of a mature culture. The Maoris paid great attention to their history and from time immemorial have taught it in the family and later at school so that today research workers can follow events back to 900 A.D. We thus know that in the 13th century the aborigines of New Zealand were strengthened by a tremendous wave of immigrants from Polynesia. Even the names of the ships in which the Polynesians came have been preserved. From them come aristocratic genealogies. The Maoris were outstanding warriors and even won the admiration of the colonizers. Today they have equal rights in the state.

Their artistic expressions were directed mainly at decoration. The sculptural works are mostly from a green stone—jade—more like jewels than works of sculptural art. The small statuettes, tiki, are hereditary family ornaments. The artistic, complicated and painful tattooing with deep scars, rubbed with dog's dung, are reflected in sculpture by likenesses in masks. The similarity consists mainly in the exact transcription of the tattoo pattern. What a different conception of a portrait! In the same spirit as tattooing high-spirited ornamental decorations were worked on stone, bone or wooden weapons, boxes, coffins and complicated wooden ornaments as well as on ritual furniture, canoes, household pillars and utensils. A similar development—painstakingness, thoughtfulness and over-accentuation of ornament which still manifests itself in the Marquesas—is also found in the cultures of the Central American Indians.

The home of the last island culture of Polynesia is in the Hawaiian Islands, probably settled during a later stage of the migration of nations. They have a gentle and pleasant climate. The Polynesian immigrants subdued the indigenous Menehune by force and knowledge and built here an island kingdom with a very stable political order and class set-up. Their care for the purity of aristocratic families often forced brothers and sisters to marry. Before 1820, King Kamehameha I united the powers of the small feudal kingdoms and entrusted their administration to feudal lords.

Apart from the small wooden statuettes of deities and the artistically worked utensils, plates and bowls for food, decorated with caricatures of their enemies, the Hawaiians chiefly concentrated their artistic powers on clothing. Coloured materials, clothes, caps, helmets and canonical dress with red and yellow birds' feathers were the most outstanding bearers of artistic feeling. Patterns printed by stamping with leaves or forms dipped in dye were the beginnings of textile art. One also admires the original styles. It was not a question of fashion but of a transfer of artistic interests to clothing. The ritual masks with birds' helmets were an important part of religious ceremonies but were made of grass or bark fibres and have not been preserved. The emphasis on clothing both of the gods and of the people finds its analogy both with the Maoris and on the Marquesas Islands but nowhere else in Oceania does it occur to such an extent. Practically nothing of the artistic works has been preserved. Of the statues, which decorated the altars in the sanctuaries of the deities, only three remain. Only in the charming custom of welcoming foreigners with floral wreaths, and in their music has a vague echo of Hawaiian culture reached our times.

Melanesia means "black islands" because the numerous aborigines of this region—the Papuans and the negroid pygmies—had the features of the Negro race.

The cultural and above all the artistic expressions of the Melanesian inhabitants are less exclusive and singular than Polynesian art. The Melanesians have more feeling. In their religion the cult of mythological beings predominates, which are an object of respect and horror in the deeply emotional inhabitants. The mysterious jungle, with colourful flora and fairy-tale colouring of the birds contributed to this sensitivity; the stormy weather, snakes and crocodiles heightened the dramatic tension in the people. Thus the ceremonies were theatrically moving, the dances had an ecstatic rhythm and passionate richness. Sensuous stimulation was aided by the chewing of betel.

All the masks, weapons, drums, shields, statues, spears, dance costumes and ritual implements, canoes and sanctuary models or so-called social houses were the object of extraordinary artistic care for they were ostentatiously used during festivities. Similarly with betel cases. Some ritual statues of the village deities reached enormous dimensions. The sculptors, working with wooden axes, and bone or shell knives, counted on effect and chose supernatural proportions. The colour and exaggeration in the lengthening of noses or limbs, for example, increased the dramatic quality of the work which, however, was more realistic and nearer to nature than Polynesian art. Human likenesses were the central theme and, being coloured with expressive curves, everywhere increased the internal artistic effect. The general grandeur, pride and majesty of the figures is often surpassed by a psychologically experienced expression which sometimes attains to very realistic likenesses, particularly in the older, archaic statues.

The most characteristic artistic expressions come from the New Caledonian Islands, a French colony from 1853 which was indomitable in its passionate martial spirit and was never quite subdued.

The architectonic decoration and role of art in the large buildings had a high artistic quality; the high decorated window-frames, the entrance and supporting pillars, threshold and beams were all carved with large, realistically truthful but abbreviated and energetic stylized forms in a hard heavy wood. On the roofs of the huts the inmates raised their carved escutcheons. The statues and masks bear all the marks of great sculptural feeling having a first-class dynamic energy and artistic value. Some of the masks are flat-nosed and some have hooked eagle beaks.

The New Hebrides, plundered, morally upset and decimated by disease by the worst scum of the white race, were once a garden of flowers, and singing birds of bright plumage, but went in eternal fear of typhoons and small earthquakes which occurred daily. These natural phenomena had their conflicting effects both on art and religion.

The striving for a higher position is connected with ritual ceremonies held on the transition from one social sphere to another. Each rite demanded the sacrifice of a statue or mask which the candidate's guarantor had to make and bring to the candidate in return for a high fee paid in pigs and bristles.

The statues of chalk, palm and teak wood, and seaweeds caked with clay, the masks and drums, all having supernaturally enlarged faces with eyes and long chins and skulls, are richly painted almost to the point of exaggeration. For night dancing the masks are also decorated with whiskers and hair, caps and clothes which give an immensely strong and dramatic effect in contrast to the silent awe of the tremendous pillar statues. From an art point of view the artists from the New Hebrides, although not all on the same level as regards abilities, rank among the most unique of the Melanesian creative workers.

The central but heterogeneous home of the origin of Melanesian artistic culture is the large island of New Guinea. The artistic expressions of the New Guinea artists are sometimes incorrectly considered to comprise an independent cultural region in Oceania. Even today not all the regions of this tremendous island have been explored and mapped. The population of mixed races and tongues formed several culturally differentiated regions in the river basins or sea gulfs. But these regions are subject to mutual influences and in the western part of the island Indonesian influences are very strong.

The most easterly tip of the island is inhabited by Melanesian immigrants, while the rest of the island population is mostly Papuans. The art of the Massine region (western) has common features with the art of the Solomon Islands and some ornamental elements similar to patterns from Marquesas.

In Papuan art primary importance is enjoyed by the carving and sculpture of the Sepik river basin, followed by art from the Fly and Purari river basins which flow into the Gulf of Papua. The works of great constructional ability and with a certain daring construction in the social ritual houses, in the centre of extensive villages, are far surpassed by the sculptural works and hideous grinning masks made from the most diverse materials—wood, shells, coral, cloth and vegetable fibres. In the flat ornament of the extremely poetical drawings, various colours and white play the role of space. The long noses in tattooed likenesses of human faces are emphasized with animal attributes almost to the point of being comic. The great variety and wealth

of invention drawn from the bird, reptile and animal kingdom, counting on the expressive effect of staring gazes, are the chief features of Papuan art which is applied to all objects of daily use—furniture, pots, seats, thrones and tables, hooks for meat and supplies. The tremendous festivities, prepared for several years, accumulated a great amount of artistic works, so that they formed a very rich basis for artistic research.

In the Torres Strait, at one time the cannibal home of head-hunters, tortoise-shell is also used as a material. In the Huon Bay stylization and a sort of artistic hardness is perhaps the first mark of decay in the national, highly dramatic art of Papua.

New Britain and particularly New Ireland are island entities with a marked sculptural feeling for a rich complication of forms together with a black, red and white sculptural colour sense.

The huge monstrous masks of New Britain and the complicated long-eared constructions of ritual equipment have an unusual appearence. In the same way as the surface-carved ornament in Marquesas and New Zealand accentuated the exaggerated curves, so in New Ireland there developed forms in complicated sculptural conceptions, in chains of birds, animals and figures one on top of the other (as in many simpler Indian totems), and in the sculptures of religious protective family deities, known as *uli*. The helmets decorated with brush bristles and woollen fibres, feathers and sea-weed are directly connected with masks from the region of monsters, apparitions, death and from the animal kingdom. These were often in the likeness of pigs and birds.

The Admiralty Islands reverted from the exuberant rhythm of the New Ireland sculpture to balanced forms, ornamentally and sculpturally more calm and monumental in their simplicity. The geometric pattern is again visible here and with a firmer art we also find a more stable social order. Some kind of currency in the form of dogs' teeth and rare shells was even introduced. The obsidian weapons and a sense for rare materials are outstandingly manifest.

The sculpture of the Solomon islands, sombre, black and shining with inlaid mother-of-pearl, attains monumentality with its coldness and sparsity of form and gesture. There is some kind of great nobleness and dignity in it which has the marks of refined elegance.

The heads from the bows of pirogues and canoes, the shields with an ornament stylized to the very core, the pure forms of pots and above all the richly-inlaid jewels made from shells and tortoise-shell, the tablets for hanging on the chest—all have the same order and sense for compactness of content in a pure and clear form.

The figures and masks, of which there are the least here of all the islands, have a typical hair-dress similar to the turban. The black colour predominates. It is supplemented by a brownish-red so that some vessels and patterns have the colour scheme of Greek vases.

Incrustation is the most typical feature of artistic work in hard wood. The concentrated expression of the faces is strengthened by the inlaid eyes, eye-lashes and tattooing.

Ship-building—*tamako*—is famed throughout Oceania. Yet another attitude, typical of the art of the Solomon Islands, is the supported head in the decoration of the bows and stern of ships. A figure sitting and thinking with his chin supported on his hand—*kokorra*—often occurs in statues.

The art of the Solomon Islands holds a special place in Melanesian art by reason of its intrinsic artistic values. Micronesia—small islands scattered over a tremendous sea area—indisputably ranks behind Melanesia

and Polynesia in its artistic and social development. Indonesian influence is the most apparent here both directly in the human faces, and in the cultivation of Asiatic rice, ship-building and sea-faring, for the Indonesians were the only ones to mature to some kind of primitive cartography of sea routes.

The first metal instruments and weapons appeared early in Micronesia, having surprisingly little influence on carving but greatly affecting the production of wooden objects and tools of daily use. Asiatic conceptions and scientific equipment and knowledge also appear in the social life of the islanders. For example, on the Carolines there were brothels for unmarried men and men's clubs existed on the Marshall Islands; there was also a knowledge of geography and navigation by means of the stars and a charting of sea currents which are exceedingly swift in this part of the world.

The Second World War, the scene of which were the coral atolls of Micronesia, the Solomon Islands (Guadalcanar and Bougainville) and New Guinea, inflicted a crushing blow to research into and a cognition of the cultures of Oceania.

Explorative research of Oceanic artistic expression took the wrong path in the last years before the war. Some studies attempted to extract the utmost from the treasures of Oceanic art for their own narrow needs and to find in Oceanic artistic expression a support for the surrealist conception of art, for subject-less painting and mystical magical philosophy. The treasures scattered throughout museums (for example the large unexhibited works of the Musée de l'homme in Paris) allow of a fairly accurate and careful study of the creative side of Oceanic art but the remoteness of the region and the expense of scientific and particularly art-scientific expeditions, make a study on the spot very difficult.

Oceanic culture is less known than famous, less understood than publicized. It is a culture, however, having a quality which stands out above all others — a predominance of fine arts in the realm of artistic expression. For this reason it is an indispensable region of study for science and the theory of fine art.

Adolf Hoffmeister

198. Head from New Mecklenburg (Tombara). Human skull covered with a layer of painted clay, shells instead of eyes, hair from vegetable fibres, height 21.5 cm., Náprstek Museum, Prague.

200. Figure of a man from New Pomerania (Birara). Light wood, hair from red bark-fibre, mother-of-pearl eyes. Height 38 cm., private collection.

201. Human figure from New Guinea—the Sepik River. Burnt wood with the remnants of clay incrustation, h. 82 cm., Prague Náprstek Museum (see No 215, 216).

202. Fetish from New Guinea—the Sepik River. Flat carving in wood, hollowed place covered with white paint. In the curves of the ornament, typical for Sepik art, are the remnants of stylization of human figures. Height 19 cm., private collection.

205. Clay vessel from New Guinea—the Sepik River. Ornament carved to great depth. Vessels used for cannibal purposes were pressed into soft soil so that a straight bottom was unnecessary. Reddish-brown colour. Imported at the end of the last century, diam. 23 cm., Náprstek Museum, Prague.

206. Figure of crocodile from Admiralty Islands. Light wood decorated with coloured plastic ornament of interlinked figures. Length 59.5 cm., private collection.

208. Bird with a snake in its beak from New Mecklenburg (Tombara). Light soft wood, entirely covered with coloured ornaments, part of architecture(?). Length 76 cm., Náprstek Museum, Prague.

211. Ornamental part of a house, in the form of fish, from New Mecklenburg (Tombara). Polychrome wood decorated with shells. Length 72 cm., Náprstek Museum, Prague.

213. Head from New Guinea—the Sepik River. Human skull covered with layer of painted clay. Hair from human pigtail, eyes of halved shells. Height 17 cm., Náprstek Museum, Prague.

214. Head of a figure from New Guinea—the Sepik River. Black incrusted wood with shells inserted in eye-sockets and bark-fibre. New Guinea, height of whole figure 34.5 cm., height of reproduced part 12 cm., Náprstek Museum, Prague.

215. Figure as in No 201 Detail of head.

216. Figure as in No 201. Detail.

217. A Taro-Beater from New Guinea—the Sepik River(?). Remnants of ornamental painting. Height 34 cm., Náprstek Museum, Prague.

218. Figure of a man from New Guinea—the Sepik River. Polychrome wood, eyes inlaid with shells, two figures of parrots on the head. Height 32.5 cm., Náprstek Museum, Prague.

219. Head-rest from New Guinea—the Sepik River. Polychrome wood decorated with shells. Height 14 cm., Náprstek Museum, Prague.

220. Figure of a man from New Guinea—the Sepik River. Wood, height 17 cm., private collection.

221. Hook in the form of a male figure from New Guinea—the Sepik River. Wood, stained red and with decorative hangings made of shells. Ornament, whiskers denoted by carving. Height 28 cm., private collection.

222. Hook in the form of a bat from New Guinea—the Sepik River. Used for hanging food out of the reach of rats. Wood. Height 11.5 cm., private collection.

223. Hook in the form of a shark from New Guinea—the Sepik River. Used as the hook in No 222. Wood, height 28 cm., private collection.

224. Paddle from Solomon Islands—Buka. Flat relief carving in hard wood, red, brown and black colouring. Length of reproduced part 96 cm., Náprstek Museum, Prague (see No 240).

225. Ornamental part of house from New Mecklenburg (Tombara). Pierced wood-carving and richly and colourfully decorated, shells inserted in eye-sockets and under outstretched arms, hair and whiskers of animal hairs. Height 86 cm., Náprstek Museum, Prague.

226. Mask from New Guinea—the Sepik River. Wood ornamentally painted and decorated with grass and bark fibre. Height 27 cm., private collection.

227. Mask from New Guinea—the Papuan Gulf. Bast, grass and tapa, height 55 cm., Náprstek Museum, Prague.

228. Shield from New Guinea—the Papuan Gulf. Wood, relief ornament derived from stylized human likeness almost completely transformed into geometric form. Brown, red and white. Sepik, New Guinea. Height 86.5 cm., Náprstek Museum, Prague.

229. Shield from New Guinea—the Sepik River. Heavy wood decorated with deep carving, one of the most beautiful pieces of its kind. Height 125 cm., Náprstek Museum, Prague.

230. Parrot from Solomon Islands(?). Probably from ship's bows, light wood, eye of transparent stone. Height 32 cm., Náprstek Museum, Prague.

231. Mask. Polychrome wood. New Guinea(?), height 35,4 cm., private collection.

232. Spear with obsidian tip from the Admiralty Islands. Wood-carving depicting the head of a crocodile swallowing a man. A fragment of volcanic glass in the turban-like covering of the head which is decorated with blue glass pearls. Complete length of weapon 163.5 cm., reproduced part 27.5 cm., private collection.

233. Spatula from New Guinea. Used during the eating of certain kinds of foods (gripped in binding of shield, where it was sometimes worn), painted wood. Length 34 cm., private collection.

234. Small mask from New Guinea—the Sepik River. Wood with shells. Height 21.5 cm., private collection.

235. Small mask from New Guinea—Sepik. Wood, height 18 cm., private collection.

236. Vessel from New Guinea—the Sepik River. Grey clay fired hard with branded white and reddish-brown colour. The vessel was turned upside down with the rounded spokes, pressed into soft soil and served cannibalistic purposes. Imported at the end of last century, diam. 24 cm., Náprstek Museum, Prague.

237. Bows of chieftain's ship from Solomon Islands—New Georgia. Heavy wood with tarsia work, mother-of-pearl for eyes and whiskers, otherwise entirely covered with black resinous coating. Height of reproduced part 20.5 cm., private collection.

238. Head-rest and bowl from New Guinea—the Sepik River. The former used for supporting the head during sleep, wood, height 16 cm.; the latter the outer part of a clay vessel for food, painted with brown and white paint, diam. 41 cm., private collection.

240. Two paddles as in No 236 and 242, detail.

241. Three sticks of unknown purpose from Eastern Islands, Solomon Islands and New Guinea. Wood, part of the central one red and white. Left from Eastern Islands, visible length 22 cm., centre from Solomon Islands, length 43 cm., right from Sepik, New Guinea, length of reproduced part 56 cm., Náprstek Museum, Prague.

242. Paddle. Detail. Wood with relief carving and polychrome (red, brown and black). Solomon Islands, Buka. Length of part seen in the picture 75 cm. Náprstek Museum, Prague.

216

219

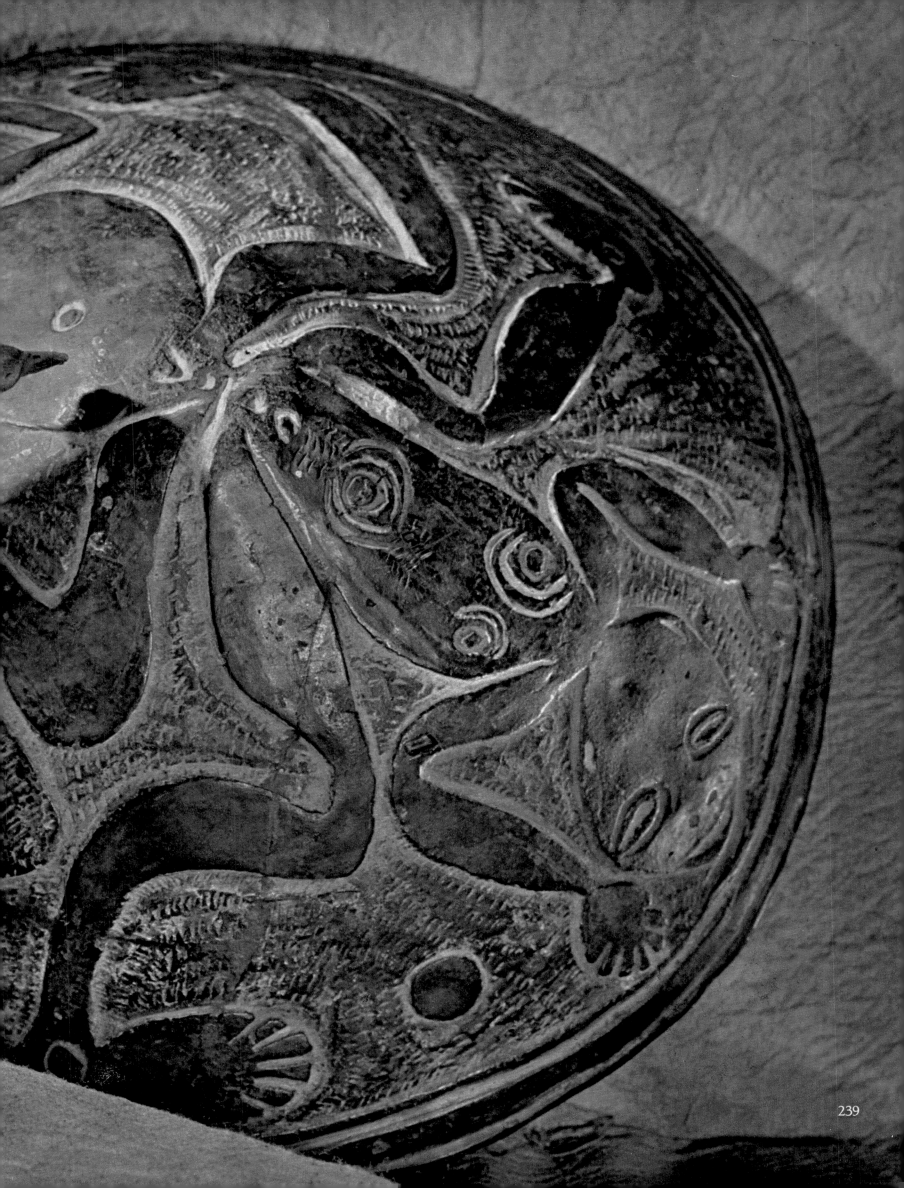

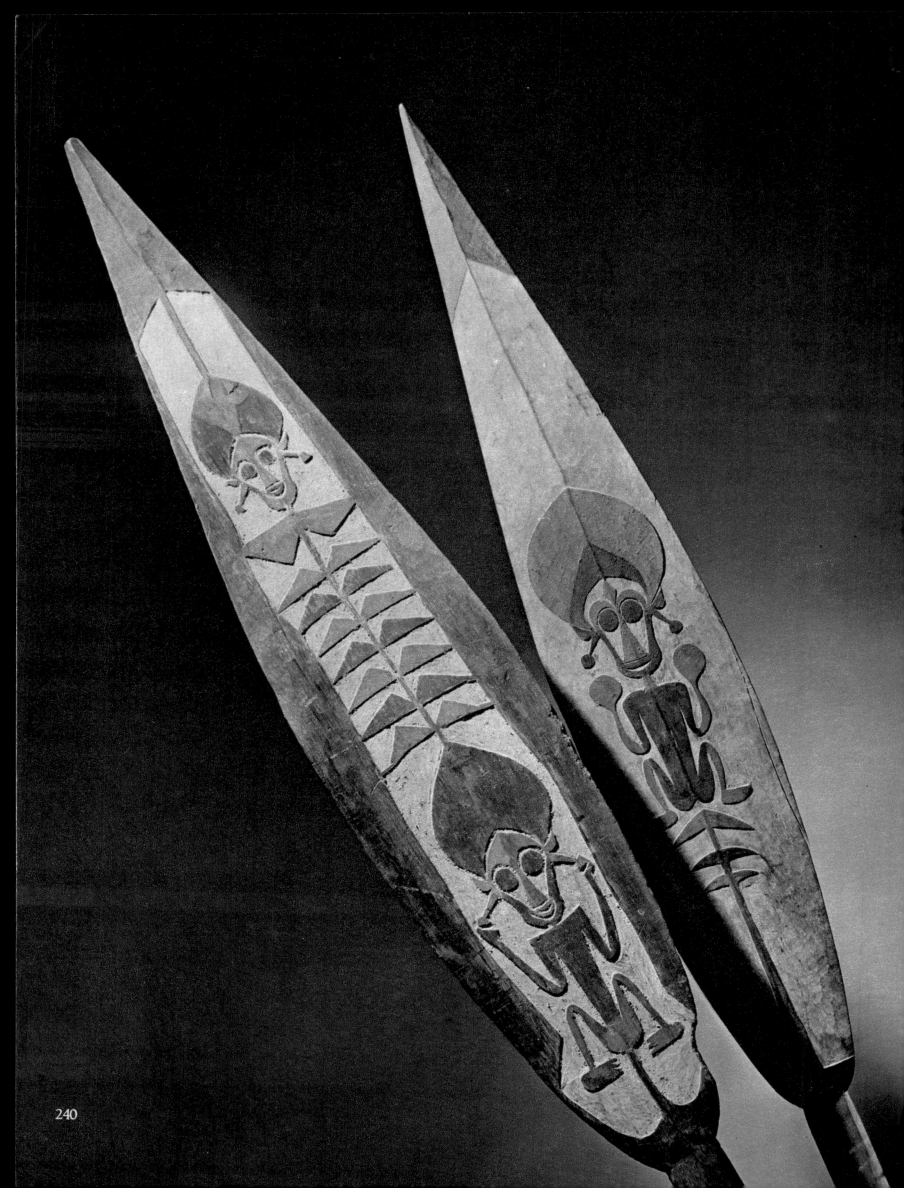

240

242

HE WAS THERE – TAAROA WAS HIS NAME
ALL ABOUT HIM WAS EMPTINESS
NOWHERE THE LAND, NOWHERE THE SKY
NOWHERE THE SEA, NOWHERE MAN
TAAROA CALLED OUT – NO ECHO TO ANSWER
THEN IN THIS SOLITUDE HE BECAME THE WORLD
THIS KNOT OF ROOTS – IT IS TAAROA
THE ROCKS – ARE HIM AGAIN
TAAROA – THE SONG OF THE SEA
TAAROA – HE NAMED HIMSELF
TAAROA – TRANSPARENCE
TAAROA – ETERNITY
TAAROA – THE POWERFUL
CREATOR OF THE UNIVERSE
WHICH IS BUT THE SHELL OF TAAROA
WHO BESTOWS IT LIFE IN BEAUTIFUL HARMONY.

From a Polynesian mythus on the creation of the world.

Indonesia

Wayang and Batik

JAVANESE WAYANG AND BATIK

It would not be correct in characterizing the art of certain nations or geographical regions to give only the so-called canonical works which have been preserved for thousands of years. The typical and specific features of a certain art cannot be comprehended if no notice is taken of the innumerable small works—the art of thousands of unknown artists from among the people, who base their work on a common denominator— national tradition. It is they who fill in the famous works of great artists, builders and thinkers by forming for them a frame, a background, the living soil.

In the art of Indonesia, and particularly of Java, such a place is held, side by side with the great Sivaist and Buddhist constructions, the world-known reliefs of Boro-Budur and Lara Djonggrang, by the work of anonymous artists who handed down their art from generation to generation. Work unpretentious and carried out in non-durable materials, not resisting the ravages of time—such is batik and the shadow theatre called *wayang-purva*. Both, as will be seen below, grew up closely connected with folk art.

It cannot be said exactly from where and when batik work and shadow plays came to Java. The shadow theatre was known under the name of Ying-hsi in China in the 10th century. At the beginning of the 11th century, the Javanese poet, Ardjunavivaha, makes first mention of shadow plays. In India the shadow theatre appeared in the 13th century.

Indian influence on Java began to make itself felt about the 1st century A. D. There are records from the 4th century which give information on the founding of individual kingdoms by Indian colonizers. Indian influences later increased, culminating in the middle of the 8th century, as is seen in the artistic relics of central Java. It can thus be assumed that even though contemporary development cannot be eliminated, the shadow theatre began in China and came to Java across India. Although there is a difference in time between the Indian and Javanese sources which apparently repudiates this thesis, it can be explained by the negligible number of preserved relics. On the other hand, it can be stated with certainty that in the period when paper was known and in general use for filling in windows in China, which stimulated the discovery of shadows on a transparent material, such conditions did not exist in Java.

With the retreat of Buddhism in the 9th century building activities gradually ceased here, moving to the east where under the increasing influence of Hinduism a number of important constructions arose. Cultural relations with India, which had been so intensive during the preceding Buddhist era, thus began to grow weaker—the typically Indian elements in style began to mingle with Indonesian elements. There thus came about a temporary symbiosis of a mature art having its roots in India with indigenous folk art of the Malayan archipelago by a complicated process lasting 400 years as a result of which the foreign elements were absorbed and the wayang style arose.

The connection between the wayang on the theatre screen and batik work on the one hand, and the greatest Buddhist constructions at their peak on the other stands out clearer if we examine only the artistic side.

the heroes of which are mythological figures from old religious legends. These figures then get from the theatrical scenes into batik patterns. Since the figures are of divine origin, batik work uses these motifs mainly for temple purposes or for the emperor's court. In this way the figures of the oldest tradition become in the broadest sense of the word the bearers of the wayang style.

The wayang style is a late style, the style of a decaying cultural epoch. As we have seen, it is the result of an interesting creative struggle and an amalgamation which reached its peak approximately five hundred years ago. It has preserved for us an artistic formulation which would have disappeared long ago if it had not passed into the sphere of ever-vital folk art.

As regards the technique of batik work, this is the decoration and dyeing of materials which in various forms is known throughout Asia. In Indonesia itself, the oldest mention of some kind of batik work is made in the Sundanese manuscript of 1518. Chinese sources reveal, however, that the fame of Indonesian textile art pertains to a much older date but it is doubtful whether this actually referred to the technique of batik work. A Chinese chronicle from the Liang Dynasty (A.D. 518) for example reports that the Prince of Bali sent emissaries to the Chinese Emperor bringing, among other gifts, a cotton robe. A later chronicle from the T'ang Dynasty (A.D. 614-906) observes that only cotton robes were worn in Java. It is not until the Sung Dynasty (A.D. 960-1279) that we read in the chronicles that a Javanese prince sent robes of silk and cotton of various colours to the Chinese ruler.

What is it that made of lowly cotton such a wonderful material, fit to be given as gifts by the highest nobles, about which chroniclers wrote and which the poets compared to the beauty of women? It was not only the fine art of painting but also a unique dyeing technique. Batik work is a long and difficult process of painting with melted wax, something similar to the painting of Easter eggs. The whole process is divided into several important phases. First the material is cut to the necessary length, hemmed, thoroughly boiled, washed and rinsed. It is then soaked in oil. The basic colour of the batik must be decided upon in this preparatory stage because this determines the type of oil bath used. For example, for a brownish red base, the cloth must be soaked in oil for about 40 days. It is steeped daily in fresh oil and lye and then carefully

We see here an interesting metamorphosis. The fully plastic figures of the Boro-Budur reliefs, in places almost detaching themselves from the background, are much finer in the next important construction Lara Djonggrang and at the same time hold more to the background; in later buildings, they recede more and more and are deprived of their corporeal substance by the deformation of their limbs until they finally become wayangs in the reliefs (now only flat fillings) of the holy Panataran. Wayangs live on unchanged in folk art today in its purest form, batik and wayang-purva.

How did Javanese batik and shadow playing become such a dominant part of folk art in Indonesia? It would be hard to answer this question completely satisfactorily in the same way as it is no easy task to explain and lift out of their context of time, social and other factors those events and conditions which give rise to any kind of folk art.

We shall give two of those factors here however, apart from others which played a substantial role such as raw materials, the most suitable vegetable pigment, climatic conditions, etc. On the one hand there is the tremendous popularity enjoyed by both these arts with the natives themselves (from the peasant to the sultan there is no more popular clothing than batik-worked cotton materials and no better amusement than the wayang theatre). On the other hand there is the mutual retrospective effect of one art on the other in the framework of respect for tradition. It should be borne in mind that the wayang is the result of centuries of tradition, superstitions and mythological teachers, in most cases supported by religious aspects.

One can thus see a direct line connecting the above-mentioned great works, the Sivaist and Buddhist temple statues, their cults, legends and rites with temple dances, the theatre, dress and thus also with batik.

What tradition means to Indonesian art and with what persistence it was kept to by the Indonesians can be seen from the fact that in a Sundanese record of 1518 mention is made of a pattern called *alas alassan* (forest animal) which today, 400 years later, is still used in Java.

In the same way that the common batik patterns depicting emblems of happiness, long life, fauna, flora and the whole of nature are handed down so are religious rites, sacrificial festivities and temple dances strictly adhered to in their original form. It is not surprising therefore if they are reflected in the wayang plays dried. The cloth is then stretched taut, the excess oil scraped off and the material beaten with big wooden sticks. This gives it a polished surface so that the most delicate designs can be made with the wax. With batik of inferior quality, the material is ironed instead of being beaten. The oil impregnation is also carried out in a much simpler and quicker way, having its effect naturally on the batik.

When the material has thus been prepared, the real batik work can start. This is almost exclusively the women's job. The desired design is lightly outlined on the oil-impregnated and polished cloth with carbon or pencil. This is either done free-hand or traced from paper patterns. During drawing the material is either placed on the floor or hung on a wooden frame. In the latter case the pattern, cut out of paper, is often held on the back side of the material, against the light, and the design outlined on the front with pencil or directly with wax.

The wax is put on the material with a special tool called the *tganting*, which is actually a sort of fountain pen. To prevent the vessel burning the cloth it is usually placed in a small bamboo wrapping.

Formerly real bee's wax was used and in order to make its consistency harder and more durable it was mixed with resin. Today specially prepared paraffin is used. All parts of the cloth, which are to contain a design and to have a different colour than the base, must be covered with wax. First the design lightly outlined in pencil is covered with wax. When all the surfaces which are to have a different colour have been covered the whole cloth is reversed and stretched on a wooden frame. On the reverse side the same areas must be covered with wax so that both sides will have exactly the same pattern and colour. The cloth is then dipped into the basic dye. Formerly this was usually blue, made from indigo, or red, made from tree bark. Indigo was used cold, while the brownish-red dye was used at a lukewarm temperature so as to dye the material better.

The art of dyeing is inseparably connected with batik work. Not only the making of the dyes but especially the dyeing itself was the work of masters. The colour of the material depended upon the skill of the dyer. This consisted not only in the different methods of dyeing but mainly in how the freshly dyed piece of cloth was exposed to the sun's rays; indigo for example only assumes its blue colour after oxidation. Nowadays such worries do not exist since batik is practically always dyed by artificial aniline dyes which are easier to use, quicker and cheaper.

When the first colour has thoroughly dried the whole cloth is washed in hot water to dissolve the wax. After this the batik begins to take on its full beauty. On the places formerly covered with wax and which were supposed to remain white, we can see tiny veins of the basic colour. This is because when the dyer submerges the cloth into the cold dye solution the wax hardens, cracks and the dye penetrates into these cracks, even on the covered parts. This blurriness and veined quality of the design and the penetration of colour under the wax is the most typical characteristic of batik work.

Additional designs are made upon the well-washed cloth and the material is dyed again. This is repeated for each colour. In manufacturing cheaper batik the old method is replaced by wooden or copper stamps which apply the wax directly to the material.

Batik has been highly valued since time immemorial; it was a material exchanged as presents between kings and princes and was a necessary adjunct of courtly raiment. It was also the material of the lowliest citizens who dressed themselves in magnificent batik sarongs and slendangs in the same way as the princes. The wife of the simplest peasant batik-worked cotton cloth in the same way as the princess; and using the same simple means she was able to create an object characterizing the artistic sense of Indonesia.

Bedřich Forman and Miroslav Oplt

246. Puppet, Wayang Golèk from Western Java. Wood, painted, gilded and lacquered, skirt of batik, dried wings, gilded buffalo skin. The conception of these puppets, dictated by the ancient iconographical canon, based on the old Indian scripts Ramayana and Mahabharata, remains the same for shadow-theatre puppets—Wayang Purwa—and the clothing of the living characters in the Wayang-Orang plays also corresponds. Height 61 cm., Náprstek Museum, Prague.

248. Cotton curtain with the Water Kingdom. Possibly from Java, gold foil applied on Bali. Blue décor with gold foil, length 225 cm., National Gallery, Prague (see Nos 264, 266).

253. Nobles on a trip, batik from Western Java. Batik on cotton, bluish-brown colour, dimensions 54.5 × 199 cm., private collection.

255. Mask for Wayang-Orang Play. Dyed and gilded wood, age unknown, height 225 cm., National Gallery in Prague.

256. Shadow-play scenery Kékayon. Wood, flatly carved in relief, pierced, dyed and gilded, sitting figure framed by two snakes, age unknown, height 35 cm., private collection.

257. Puppet Wayang Purwa. Wood with faint relief finish, painted and gilded; ear-rings and diadem decorated with pieces of glass, age unknown, height 38.8 cm., private collection.

258. Batik with boat and fish motif from Western Java. Banana fibre(?) with brown drawing on greyish-blue background, dimensions 225 × 110 cm., private collection.

260. Batik with figural scene from Central Java. Cotton, blue and brown colour, dimensions 102 × 88 cm., National Gallery, Prague.

261. Batik with demon and serpent from Western Java(?). Cotton, dark blue and brown colour, dimensions 103 × 150 cm., private collection.

262. Batik with three demons from Central Java. Cotton having yellow basic colour, brownish-blue painting, dimensions 109.5 × 91 cm., private collection.

264. Water Kingdom. Detail from curtain of No 248.

266. Fishes. Detail from the curtain of No 248.

267. Two Kris-Knives from Bali. Hilt carved from ivory, left one beautifully decorated with gold. 16th-17th century(?), length of hilt 9.5 cm., Prague Náprstek Museum and private collection.

268. Two Kris-Knives from Bali. The hilt of the left one ivory and gold, inlaid with semi-precious stones, the right one from pure gold, inlaid with semi-precious stones. 16th-17th century(?). Length of left 45 cm. (hilt alone 13 cm.), length of right 45 cm. (hilt alone 15 cm.), private collection.

270. Raksassa, God-Demon from Bali. Hammered silver, 18th-19th century(?), height of whole figure 20 cm., batik in background, private collection.

271. Wood-sculpture from Bali. Hard wood, remnants of red and white paint, 17th-19th century, height 80 cm., Náprstek Museum, Prague (see Nos 272, 273).

272. Wood-sculpture as in No 271. Detail.

273. Wood-sculpture as in No 273, detail of head of upper figure.

274. Figure carved in tortoise-shell. Here too the wayang feature is preserved although the figure is probably not a mythical being. Provenience and age indefinite, height 18 cm., private collection. Batik sarong in background.

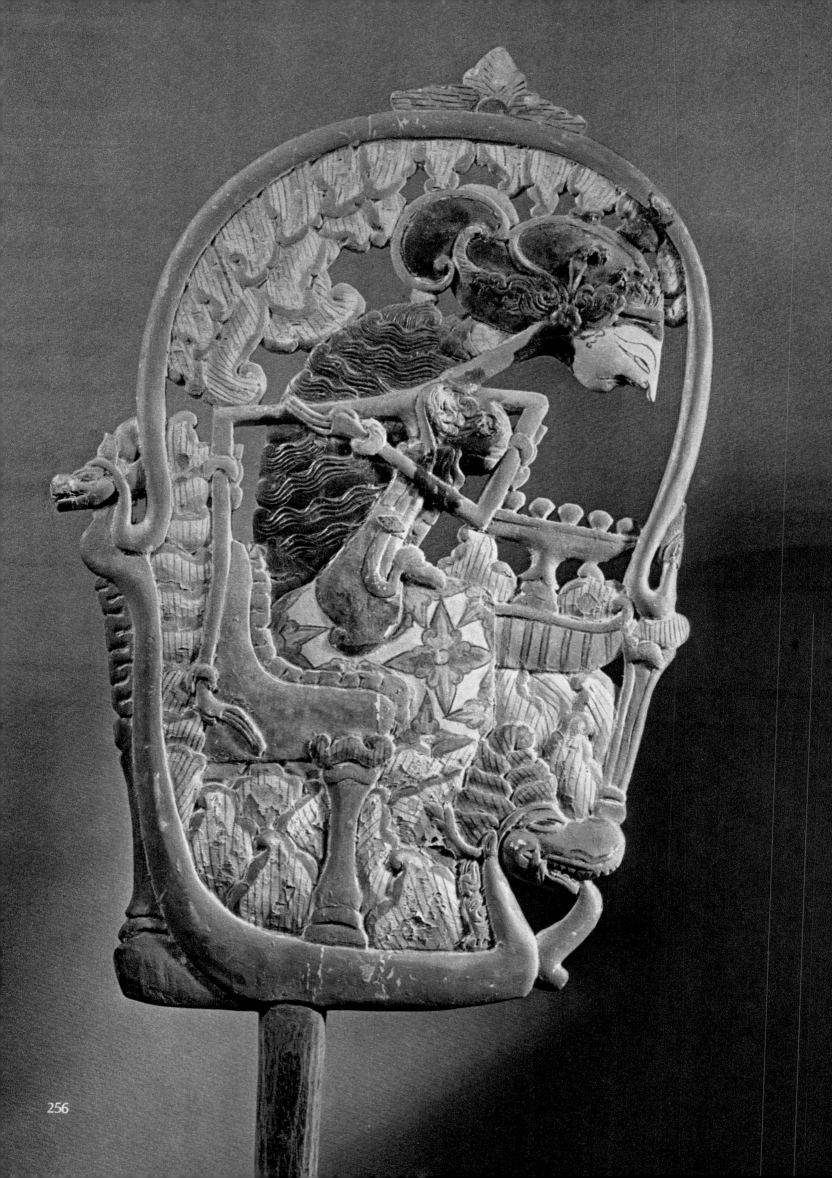

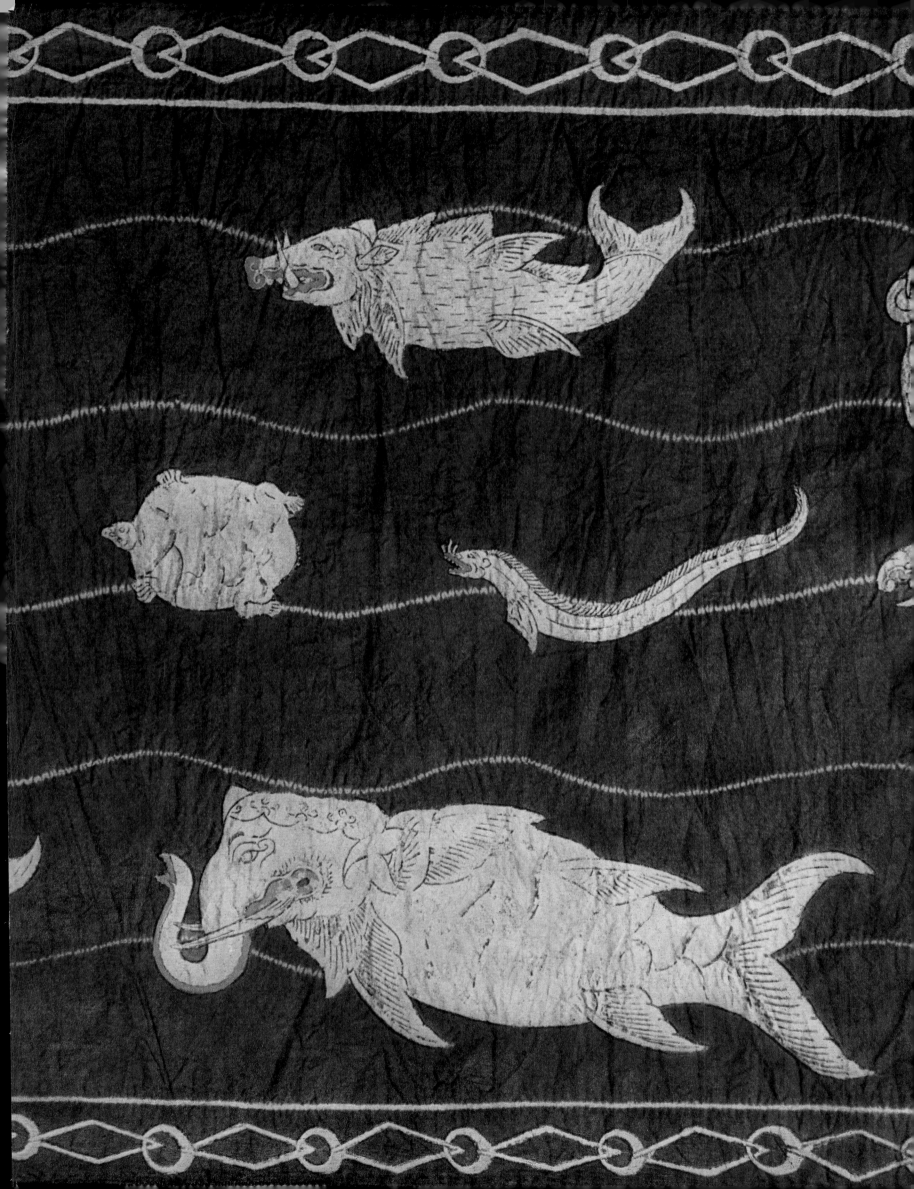

270

WHAT IS A BRIGHT COLOURED SCARF TO ME
IF IT IS BLACK AS BLACK CAN BE WITH DIRT
WHAT IS A PRETTY WIFE TO ME
IF ON SUNDAY SHE CHEATS ME JUST AS ALL WEEK

Malayan pantun.

Indonesia

The Bataks

TUNGAL-PANALOAN

Protected by impenetrable jungle and above all by their firm stand against the colonization attempts of white men, the Bataks were, until the beginning of the 20th century, able to live their lives in North Sumatra untouched by European civilization. Only the 20th century, and in particular the Second World War, put an end to this. Today airplanes regularly land in Sumatra and the old customs and rituals have become merely interesting spectacles for sensation-seeking tourists. Perhaps only in the heart of the tropical jungles or in the deepest corners of the heart of a handful of natives something has been preserved of that which. five decades ago, formed the core of Batak culture.

We know that until recently the Bataks and some of their neighbouring tribes were cannibals. Several cases are known of a white man having been put to death and eaten. In addition to these cases which have been punished by penal expeditions sent out by the Dutch authorities, there have been many instances of cannibalism during wars among the natives themselves. Such cases are not even recorded because they do not come under the jurisdiction of the occupation forces but the countless skulls which are used to decorate the huts of native warriors bear witness to this. It must be pointed out that cannibalism among the Bataks was not a result of physical need. It was a punishment, in fact the final stage of an accomplished punishment.

The Bataks believed, together with other aboriginal peoples, that the power, strength, wisdom and all the other attributes possessed by their enemy were transformed to them when they ate him. From the pillories on which the condemned were fastened for the execution, the Bataks fashioned curiously carved wands. With these the local medicine man, *data*, increased his power over his fellow tribesmen, pretending that these wands had supernatural qualities which could cure, wound or even conquer the enemy in war. From this comes their name, *tungal-panaloan*, which means "the wand which gives victory."

These wands are interesting not only for their wood-carving, but also for their artistic conception. Despite the fact that they are much sought after for exhibition in public or private collections very little is known of the history, or rather the legend, which gives rise to this curious philosophy. Generally it is erroneously confused with the totem carvings of the Indians of north-western America or similar work by certain African tribes. At first glance they may seem to have a lot in common but this feature is only of a formal basis, in that the figures of men and beasts are carved one above the other so that they form a column or staff.

The legend referred to above is interesting not only for the motifs which are depicted in the carvings, but also in that at the same time it gives an insight into the tribal legislation and ethic conceptions of the Batak peoples.

We are informed that many years ago there lived a brother and sister, the ancestors of the Batak people, on the northern shore of Lake Tobak. Then, the same as now, adultery and incest were punishable by death. The brother and sister, who married each other, fled into the jungle to escape this punishment. After wandering for a long time they were forced to look for food. The woman climbed a tree to pick some fruit (as with almost all

other primitive peoples, it was the woman who did all the heavy work and who prepared the food). She threw down the fruit but was unable herself to descend. She was caught in the branches. Her brother and husband wanted to help her but he, too, was caught in the tree which held them fast. The unhappy couple were fed by animals and birds of the jungle, all of whom fell in the tree's clutches.

Among their would-be rescuers was a holy bird, a *tucon*, called the *Buk-buk* which, with his clear, twice-repeated call, "tiling dong, tiling dong," called for human help. The tree was attacked by humans, reptiles, birds and animals but all were caught in its toils so that finally the tree was enveloped by bodies moving in a wild melange, trying desperately to escape. When even the chieftain himself (generally represented on the wand as the largest figure on horse-back) was unable to help and was also held, the *datu* set out on the following night to cut down the tree and thus obtain the most powerful *tungal-panaloan*.

The Bataks are not only expert wood-carvers. They also excel in building, weaving and even in iron moulding and are remarkably mature technically. Their brass miniatures are perhaps among the best works of the primitive peoples of this region. In addition to their buildings which are outstanding among primitive nations, especially for the beautifully shaped roofs, they also involuntarily set up a lasting monument with their iron mouldings in which they liked to depict their houses and barns.

These miniatures are never more than a few dozen centimetres high and down to the smallest detail are accurate copies of the real buildings they were meant to depict. They were made by a difficult technical process combining several artistic skills and ending by pouring into a form.

The small monuments of former architecture clearly bespeak the artistic maturity of their creators and will probably still be promulgating its glory even after civilization has swallowed up the last remnants of this folk culture.

Bedřich Forman

278. The head of a rider on a three-horned buck from Northern Sumatra. Carving in hard wood. Height of whole statue 34 cm., height of reproduced part 14 cm., private collection.

280. Tungal-Panaloan from Northern Sumatra. Wood decorated with human hair and a cock's feather. The Bataks believed that with this wand the production of which required human sacrifice, they could heal the sick, call down destruction, or conjure up protective forces. Height of whole stick 135 cm., private collection.

283. Rider, as in No 278, profile.

284. Rider, as in No 278.

285. Fetish from Sumatra. Wood and bark (head of bird and pigtail of rider), denoting a mythological scene. Above: rider on horseback, the Buk-buk bird, a woman's figure, two serpents and two other human figures. Height of whole fetish 66.5 cm., visible part 45 cm., private collection.

286. Fetish, as in No 285, profile.

287. Tungal-Panaloan, as in No 280, detail.

288. Buceros Bird from Borneo. Wood-carving, height 47 cm., length 68 cm., private collection.

290. Batak magical instrument from Sumatra. Writing on bamboo case and drawings on bone blade. Height of blade 16 cm., Náprstek Museum, Prague.

292. Wand with magic inscription from Northern Sumatra. Bamboo and wood, ikkat cloth in background, height of stick 193 cm., dimensions of cloth 246 × 180 cm., private collection.

294. Head of stick. See No 292; reproduced part 38 cm., private collection.

295. Model of granary from North-East Sumatra (sometimes used as an oil lamp), faithfully depicting a real granary; brass cast in lost form, height 22 cm., private collection.

296. Model of dwelling from Northern Sumatra. Indigenous work faithfully depicting native architecture. Brass cast in lost form, height 31 cm., width 34 cm., private collection.

283

284

287

294

296

LIGHT AS THE BUTTERFLY YOU GUIDE THE BOAT THROUGH THE
WAVES
AND NONE CAN SEE HOW TIRED YOU ARE
LIKEWISE DO HIDE YOUR PAIN IN YOUR HEART
THAT NONE MIGHT KNOW YOUR WISH OR YOUR FEAR

A song from Sumatra.

Indonesia

Nias

THE NIAS COLLECTION OF P. DURDÍK

On the 26th of May, 1843, a son by the name of Pavel was born to Alois Durdík from Hořice, master hat-maker. This son, the second of 15 children, after completing his studies in general medicine at Prague and Leipzig, departed for Russia in 1868 where he worked for nine years as a renowned physician. Returning to his country, he accepted the post of military surgeon in the Dutch East Indies in the same year. There he worked for six years on the various islands and compiled his ethnographical, sociological and scientific notes in several publications. In addition to these works Czechoslovak ethnography is indebted to him for one of the most important collections of native art from the Malayan archipelagos. It comprises several dozen selected wood carvings from the island of Nias located near the western coast of Sumatra.

Nias . . . that strange island with a ringing name . . . as though its very utterance would reveal the secrets and wonders of its ancient culture.

Nias . . . a beautiful name, but does it not ring somewhat hard and sharp? Just as beautiful and severe and angular as the art creations of its people . . . just as beautiful and severe as its religious and cult ceremonials. Even the people themselves, although tall, slender and agile, have that conspicuously harsh and angular appearance in their dressing, ceremonial costumes and all their pointed and sharp decorations.

We may say that the art on this island is monochromatic. We find neither the bright radiant colours of nearby Indonesia nor the strange and somewhat terrifying designs of Oceania. It is a monochromatic and monotonous art even in its general features and shapes of block-like qualities. It is full of mystic shadows, mysterious charm, demons, gods and idols. It is charged with the presentiment of some supernatural power. The supernaturalism itself is frozen into forms rigid and static, never savagely animated, never with the gesture or motion of fear and joy. Everywhere a deathlike calm. Everywhere an icy ghostliness.

All of these fetishes, idols, figures of gods and, especially, figurines of ancestors are like hewn tree trunks with their branches cut off. Most of them could have originated from some primeval prototype of the first crude attempt to fashion the shape of a being on a piece of tree. The great majority of them indeed exhibit a marked similarity to a branching tree trunk, and hence the deduction of a common starting point.

It is especially evident on the large Y-shaped idols found in front of the houses in central and south Nias, more so than can be judged from our illustrations. Even the architecture is replete with mystic geometric elements. The houses stand in enclosures which are set against each other at an angle; and inside the houses of the chieftains the mural drawings display the same forms, traces of which are still to be found on the early stone remains. This iconographic idiom which predominates in all art works is probably as old as the culture itself. The insular character of the art then explains its faithful use for hundreds of years.

Our photographs illustrate some of the figures of idols in the collection of Dr. Pavel Durdík, deposited today in the Náprstek Museum. It is impossible to state with certainty what rank in the pantheon of Niassian gods each of them holds. Even a modest attempt to classify them would meet with extraordinary difficulty, for the native system of gods would hardly permit it. However, we may say very generally and with many reservations that the figurines bound to each other or to wooden beams denote dead ancestors (whose souls are the enemies of the living and are therefore restrained) and that the free figures suggest in part gods and in part those spirits of the dead ancestors who by some supposedly good deed or omen demonstrated their loyalty and therefore could be released.

In its entirety and in details the Durdík collection bears out the point that the severe and angular quality of the Niassian carvings spoken of in the introduction as well as their monotony do not detract from their effectiveness. Indeed, in some of the carvings it is possible to speak of the individual physiognomy of the faces which is best brought out by the sensitive eye of the camera (see Plate No 308, 309).

Bedřich Forman

300. Adu. Adu is the native term for imaginary spirits of dead ancestors. According to the conception of the natives these spirits represent semi-divine beings possessing power over the living. Carving in hard palm wood, eyes of inserted fragments (possibly from European dishes), brought home in 1884 by Dr. Durdík, height 53 cm., Náprstek Museum, Prague.

302. Adu. Black incrusted wood with typical branching on the head. Brought home in 1884 by Dr. Durdík, height 31 cm., Náprstek Museum, Prague. See No 308.

304. Series of bound Adus. Bamboo and palm wood. Brought home in 1884 by Dr. Durdík, height 108 cm., Náprstek Museum, Prague.

307. Adu. Probably a depiction of a woman ancestor with children. Light wood with fabric. Series of bound Adus in the background. Brought home in 1884 by Dr. Durdík, height 42 cm., Náprstek Museum, Prague.

308. Group of Adu figures. (See Nos 302, 324).

309. Head of Adu. Incrusted wood and fabric. The right ear lobe is broken through, a typical tiara is on the head, and there is no beard under the nose and on the chin but, instead of these, the decorations of a warrior. Brought home in 1884 by Dr. Durdík, height of the entire figure 18 cm., of the head with the tiara 8.5 cm., Náprstek Museum, Prague.

310. Group of Adu figures. Interior of a native model of a North Nias dwelling with living room, some kind of guest room in background. Width of visible part 26 cm. Brought home in 1884 by Dr. Durdík. Náprstek Museum, Prague.

312. Adu. Seldom in art does there occur a sculpture of such primitive shape as this (cf. Adu Farungu of Nos 317 and 322). Light wood, height 28 cm., brought home in 1884 by Dr. Durdík, Náprstek Museum, Prague.

313. Adu. Figure of a woman Adu. It is interesting in the sense that it belongs to a rare type of squatting Adus (the arms embrace the flexed knees). In the background a group of Adu figures. Height 32 cm., private collection.

314. Several Adus bound to a beam. Heavily incrusted, the second figure from the left is partially destroyed by insects. Maximum height 16-21 cm., brought home in 1884 by Dr. Durdík, Náprstek Museum, Prague.

316. Adu. Light wood with fabric. Bound Adus in the background. Height 58 cm., brought home in 1884 by Dr. Durdík. Náprstek Museum, Prague.

317. Adu Farungu. Charm against small pox. The expressiveness reminds one almost of the art of the mammoth hunters. Light wood, height 38 cm., brought home in 1884 by Dr. Durdík, Náprstek Museum, Prague. See Nos 312 and 322.

318. Adu of three children and husband and wife symbolically pierced by a peg, again denoting a child(?). Light wood and bark, height of the left group 12 cm., height of the right 18.5 cm., brought home in 1884 by Dr. Durdík, Náprstek Museum, Prague.

320. Seated Adu. Wood heavily incrusted and fragments of fabric. Height 18 cm., brought home in 1884 by Dr. Durdík, Náprstek Museum Prague.

321. Two bound Adus. Wood, fabric and bark, height 19.5 cm., brought home in 1884 by Dr. Durdík, Náprstek Museum, Prague.

322. Adu. Wood, height 31 cm., brought home in 1884 by Dr. Durdík, Náprstek Museum, Prague.

323. Two Adus. Carving in wood heavily incrusted with dirt and soot. Brought home in 1884 by Dr. Durdík, height 29.5 cm., Prague Náprstek Museum.

324. Three Adus. Wood, fabric and bast. Brought home in 1884 by Dr. Durdík, Náprstek Museum, Prague.

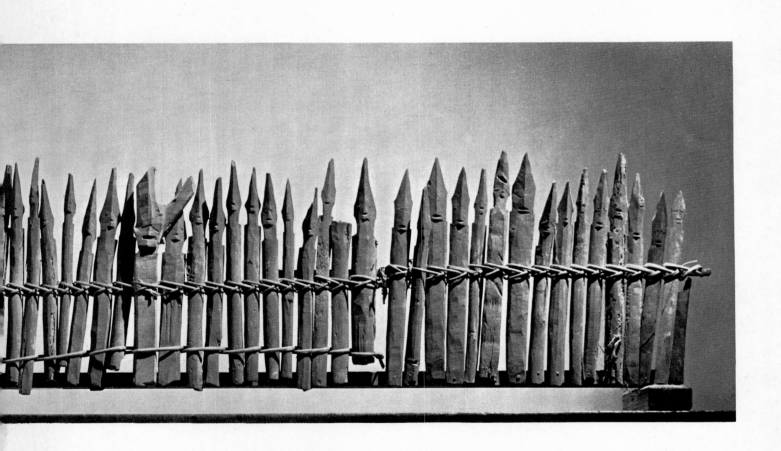

314

317

318

319

322

323

THE ANCESTOR OF THE GODS AROSE
HE WENT TO BATHE AND ANOINT HIS BODY
HE WENT TO BATHE AND OIL HIS BODY
ON THE BANK OF THE BROOK GLEAMING LIKE A SHERD
ON THE BANK OF THE BROOK GLEAMING LIKE GLASS
HE TOOK A LUMP OF CLAY AS BIG AS A FIST
HE TOOK A LUMP OF CLAY AS BIG AS AN EGG
AND BROUGHT IT TO THE VILLAGE TO THE CHIEFTAIN'S HOUSE
AND BROUGHT IT TO THE VILLAGE TO HIS OWN HOUSE
THERE THIS LUMP OF CLAY AS BIG AS A FIST
THERE THIS LUMP OF CLAY AS BIG AS AN EGG
HE KNEADED INTO THE SHAPE OF AN IMAGE
HE KNEADED INTO THE SHAPE OF A CHILD
AND THEN HE PUT IT AGAINST THE LIPS OF HIS MOUTH
AND THEN HE PUT IT AGAINST THE BREATH OF HIS MOUTH
AND THIS LUMP OF CLAY SPOKE LIKE A MAN
AND THIS LUMP OF CLAY SPOKE LIKE A CHILD
UP THERE BEFORE THE ANCESTOR OF THE GODS
AND THEN HE GAVE IT A NAME
HE GAVE IT A NAME WHICH WAS THIS
SIHÁI THE ONE WITHOUT POSTERITY
SIHÁI THE CHILDLESS ONE.

From a Niasian epic on the creation of the world.

Designed and produced by Artia for
SPRING BOOKS
Spring House · Spring Place · London NW 5
Printed in Czechoslovakia